Focus in Prekindergarten–Grade2
Teaching with Curriculum Focal Points

Focus in Prekindergarten–Grade 2

Teaching with Curriculum Focal Points

Pre-K–2

Amy Mirra

NCTM

NATIONAL COUNCIL OF
TEACHERS OF MATHEMATICS

Copyright © 2009 by
THE NATIONAL COUNCIL OF TEACHERS OF MATHEMATICS, INC.
1906 Association Drive, Reston, VA 20191-1502
(703) 620-9840; (800) 235-7566; www.nctm.org
All rights reserved

Library of Congress Cataloging-in-Publication Data

Mirra, Amy.

Focus in prekindergarten–grade 2 : teaching with curriculum focal points / Amy Mirra.

p. cm.

Includes bibliographical references.

ISBN 978-0-87353-624-0

1. Mathematics—Study and teaching (Preschool) —United States—Standards. 2. Education, Preschool—Curricula—United States—Standards. 3. Curriculum planning—United States—Standards. I. Title. II. Title: Focus in prekindergarten–grade two.

QA135.6.M5665 2009

372.7'044—dc22

2009016788

The National Council of Teachers of Mathematics is a public voice of mathematics education, providing vision, leadership, and professional development to support teachers in ensuring mathematics learning of the highest quality for all students.

Printed in the United States of America

Contents

Contents — Continued

On September 12, 2006, the National Council of Teachers of Mathematics released *Curriculum Focal Points for Prekindergarten through Grade 8 Mathematics: A Quest for Coherence* to encourage discussions at the national, state, and district levels on the importance of designing a coherent school mathematics curriculum focusing on the important mathematical ideas at each grade level. The natural question that followed the release of *Curriculum Focal Points* was "How do we translate this view of a focused curriculum into classroom practice?"

Focus in Prekindergarten–Grade 2, one of a series of three grade-band publications, is designed to support teachers, supervisors, and coordinators as they begin the discussion of a more focused curriculum across and within kindergarten through eighth grade, as presented in *Curriculum Focal Points*. Additionally, teacher educators should find it useful as a vehicle for exploring issues involving the prekindergarten–grade 2 mathematics curriculum with their preservice teachers.

The members of the development team, all active professional development leaders, designed a detailed outline for this book. We highlighted the need for new depth and coherence within the content at each grade level (prekindergarten, kindergarten, grade 1, and grade 2); the importance of connections across the content areas in prekindergarten–grade 2; and implications for learning, practice, and assessment suggested by a focused curriculum. The author of *Focus in Prekindergarten–Grade 2*, guided by our outline, created this grade-band book as a framework for lesson-study-type experiences that involve identifying focus in an existing curriculum or creating focus in a curriculum that is soon to be under revision.

Our intention for this publication is that it will be a model for professional development that supports the implementation of a more coherent and focused mathematics curriculum by posing questions that facilitate discussion and decision making. Whether you engage in reflective discussions with your colleagues or simply use these questions to stimulate independent reflection on your own instructional planning, we hope that your thinking leads you to a view of elementary school mathematics teaching that fosters in all students the depth of understanding of important mathematical concepts necessary for their future success.

—*Jane F. Schielack, for the*
CFP Grade-Band Books Development Team

As states and local school districts implement more rigorous assessment and accountability systems, teachers often face long lists of mathematics topics or learning expectations to address at each grade level, with many topics repeating from year to year. Lacking clear, consistent priorities and focus, teachers stretch to find the time to present important mathematical topics effectively and in depth.

The National Council of Teachers of Mathematics (NCTM) is responding to this challenge by presenting *Curriculum Focal Points for Prekindergarten through Grade 8 Mathematics: A Quest for Coherence*. Building on *Principles and Standards for School Mathematics* (NCTM 2000), this new publication is offered as a starting point in a dialogue on what is important at particular levels of instruction and as an initial step toward a more coherent, focused curriculum in this country.

The writing team for *Curriculum Focal Points for Prekindergarten through Grade 8 Mathematics* consisted of nine members, with at least one university-level mathematics educator or mathematician and one pre-K–8 classroom practitioner from each of the three grade bands (pre-K–grade 2, grades 3–5, and grades 6–8). The writing team examined curricula from multiple states and countries as well as a wide array of researchers' and experts' writings in creating a set of focal points for pre-K–grade 8 mathematics.

On behalf of the Board of Directors, we thank everyone who helped make this publication possible.

Cathy Seeley
President, 2004–2006
National Council of Teachers of Mathematics

Francis (Skip) Fennell
President, 2006–2008
National Council of Teachers of Mathematics

Members of the Curriculum Focal Points for Grades PK–8 Writing Team

Jane F. Schielack, *Chair*, Texas A&M University, College Station, Texas
Sybilla Beckman, University of Georgia, Athens, Georgia
Randall I. Charles, San José State University (emeritus), San José, California
Douglas H. Clements, University at Buffalo, State University of New York, Buffalo, New York
Paula B. Duckett, District of Columbia Public Schools (retired), Washington, D.C.
Francis (Skip) Fennell, McDaniel College, Westminster, Maryland
Sharon L. Lewandowski, Bryant Woods Elementary School, Columbia, Maryland
Emma Treviño, Charles A. Dana Center, University of Texas at Austin, Austin, Texas
Rose Mary Zbiek, The Pennsylvania State University, University Park, Pennsylvania

Staff Liaison
Melanie S. Ott, National Council of Teachers of Mathematics, Reston, Virginia

ACKNOWLEDGMENTS

The National Council of Teachers of Mathematics and the author would like to thank the following individuals of the CFP (Curriculum Focal Points) Grade-Band Books Development Team for developing an outline for the structure and content of this series of books. The author especially thanks Janie Schielack for all her time and support, her invaluable guidance and advice, and her continuing commitment to the Curriculum Focal Points project. We also extend a special thanks to Karen Fuson, Northwestern University, and Sybilla Beckmann, University of Georgia, for providing ideas and material for the content of this publication, as well as reviews of the manuscript.

CFP Grade-Band Books Development Team

Jane F. Schielack, *Chair*
Texas A&M University

Bonnie Ennis
Wicomico County (Maryland) Board of Education

Susan Friel
University of North Carolina

Steve Klass
San Diego State University

We would also like to thank Richard Askey, University of Wisconsin—Madison; Francis (Skip) Fennel, NCTM Past President; and James Rubillo, NCTM Executive Director, for their thoughtful reviews of, and helpful comments on, the manuscript. The final product reflects the editorial and design expertise of Ann Butterfield, NCTM senior editor, and Randy White, NCTM production manager.

Introduction

The Purpose of This Guide

Your first question when looking at NCTM's Curriculum Focal Points might be "How can I use NCTM's Focal Points with the local and state curriculum I am expected to teach?" The intent of this guide is to help instructional leaders and classroom teachers build focus into the curriculum that they are expected to teach through connecting related ideas and prioritizing topics of emphasis at each grade level. NCTM's *Curriculum Focal Points* documents are not intended to be a national curriculum but have been developed to help bring more consistency to mathematics curricula across the country. Collectively, they constitute a framework of how curricula might be organized at each grade level, prekindergarten through grade 8. They are also intended to help bring about discussion within and across states and school districts about the important mathematical ideas to be taught at each grade level. Because of the current variation among states' curricula, the Curriculum Focal Points are not likely to match up perfectly with any state curriculum. This volume, a guide to the Focal Points for prekindergarten–grade 2, explores instruction that supports a focused curriculum, as well as looks at the impact of Focal Points on assessment. Additional grade-level books for each grade band will be developed by NCTM to help teachers translate the Focal Points identified for their grade level into coherent and meaningful instruction. Taken together, this grade-band guide for prekindergarten–grade 2 and the individual grade-level books for prekindergarten, kindergarten, grade 1, and grade 2 can be used for teachers' professional development experiences, as well as by individual classroom teachers.

The Purpose of Curriculum Focal Points

The mathematics curriculum in the United States has often been characterized as "a mile wide and an inch deep." In addition, because education has always been locally controlled in the United States, learning expectations can significantly differ by state and local school systems. Many topics are studied each year—often reviewing much that was covered in previous years—and little depth is added each time the topic is addressed. In contrast, higher performing countries tend to carefully select a few fundamental topics each year and develop them in greater depth.

In the 1980s, the National Council of Teachers of Mathematics (NCTM) began the process of bringing about change to school mathematics programs, particularly with the first document to outline standards in mathematics, titled *Curriculum and Evaluation Standards for School Mathematics* (NCTM 1989). This document provided major direction to states and school districts in developing their curricula. NCTM's *Principles and Standards for School Mathematics* (2000) further elaborated on the ideas of the 1989

> *A curriculum is more than a collection of activities: It must be coherent, focused on important mathematics, and well articulated across the grades.*
>
> —The Curriculum Principle, *Principles and Standards for School Mathematics*

> The intent of this guide is to help instructional leaders and classroom teachers build focus into the curriculum that they are expected to teach through connecting related ideas and prioritizing topics of emphasis at each grade level.

Standards, outlining learning expectations in the grade bands of prekindergarten–grade 2, grades 3–5, grades 6–8, and grades 9–12. *Principles and Standards* also highlighted six Principles, which included the Curriculum Principle, to provide guidance for developing mathematics programs. The Curriculum Principle emphasized the need to link with, and build on, mathematical ideas as students progress through the grades, deepening their mathematical knowledge over time.

NCTM's *Curriculum Focal Points for Prekindergarten through Grade 8 Mathematics: A Quest for Coherence* (2006) is the next step in helping states and local districts refocus their curricula. It provides an example of a focused and coherent curriculum in prekindergarten through grade 8 by identifying the most important mathematics topics or "Focal Points" at each grade level. The Focal Points are not discrete topics to be taught and checked off, but rather a cluster of related knowledge, skills, and concepts. By organizing and prioritizing curriculum and instruction in prekindergarten–grade 8 around Focal Points at each grade level, teachers can foster more cumulative learning of mathematics by students, and students' work in the later grades will build on and deepen what they learned in the earlier grades. Organizing mathematics content in this way will help ensure a solid mathematical foundation for high school mathematics and beyond.

> **It provides an example of a focused and coherent curriculum in prekindergarten through grade 8 by identifying the most important mathematics topics or "Focal Points" at each grade level.**

The Impact of Focal Points on Curriculum, Instruction, and Assessment

Significant improvement can be made in the areas of curriculum, instruction, and assessment by identifying Focal Points at each grade level. At the curriculum level, Focal Points will allow for more rigorous and in-depth study of important mathematics at each grade level. This rigor will translate to a more meaningful curriculum that students can understand and apply, thereby ensuring student learning and an increase in student achievement. At the instructional level, Focal Points will allow teachers to more fully know the core topics they are responsible for teaching. Teachers will not necessarily be teaching *less* or *more* but will be able to teach *better*. Professional development can also be tailored to deepen teachers' knowledge of these Focal Points and connect these ideas in meaningful ways. Assessments can be designed that truly measure student mastery of core topics rather than survey a broad range of disparate topics, thus allowing for closer monitoring of student achievement. At the classroom assessment level, having a smaller number of essential topics will help teachers determine what their students have learned and provide sufficient time to ensure that those topics have been learned deeply enough to use and build on in subsequent years. Because of the extremely interconnected structure of mathematics, deeply learning the Focal Point topics at each grade level is crucial for students to be able to learn subsequent Focal Points and make the important connections among various mathematical ideas. If state assessments are more focused as well, more detailed information can be gathered for districts and schools on areas for improvement.

Focusing Curriculum

Questions to Reflect On

- **What does it mean to progress rather than "spiral" in learning?**
- **What are some of the major learning progressions that occur in prekindergarten–grade 2?**
- **How are basic facts and algorithms addressed in a focused curriculum?**

Teachers in the elementary and middle grades may feel overwhelmed with the wide range of mathematical topics expected to be taught over a given year. Pressure to cover all these topics and also prepare students for mandated state assessments is usually a major concern for many teachers. NCTM's Curriculum Focal Points are not intended to add to the already long list of concepts and skills presented in your state and local curriculum. Instead, the Focal Points can be used along with this guide to focus your own curriculum on major areas of emphasis at each grade level.

The Concept of a Focal Point and Connections

A mathematics curriculum organized around Focal Points highlights the most important mathematical ideas for each grade and presents these essential ideas as interconnected packages of related knowledge, skills, and concepts. Students gain extended experiences with these core concepts and skills with the ultimate goal of promoting a deeper mathematical understanding and connections among mathematical ideas. The majority of instruction is organized around the identified Focal Points for that grade; however, this emphasis does not mean that those focus areas are the only topics presented during that year. NCTM's Focal Points also include "Connections with the Focal Points," which are related ideas and concepts that connect with the Focal Points identified. The Connections help build relationships among mathematical ideas as well as provide meaningful contexts of study. For example, although Measurement and Data Analysis is not a Focal Point in grade 1, it connects with the Number and Operations Focal Points in this particular grade as students represent measurements and discrete data in picture and bar graphs. Such activities involve counting and comparisons that strengthen students' sense of number relationships. The Connections also serve a few other purposes. First, the Connections might highlight introductory experiences for a particular grade level to build a foundation for a Focal Point in a future grade. For example, students in grade 2 develop initial understandings of multiplication as joining equal groups using repeated addition in preparation for the grade 3 Focal Point related to basic multiplication and division facts. Connections can also serve to highlight continuing experiences of a Focal Point identified at a previous level. For example, students in grade 3 extend their understanding of place-value concepts focused on in grade 2 to numbers up to 10,000. See Appendixes A, B, C, and D for the complete listing and descriptions of the Curriculum Focal Points and Connections identified by NCTM for prekindergarten, kindergarten, grade 1, and grade 2. The Curriculum Focal Points for other grades, as well as the complete document *Curriculum Focal Points for Prekindergarten through Grade 8 Mathematics,* can be viewed on NCTM's Web site at www.nctm.org or ordered for purchase.

BUILDING-FOCUS TASK: *Think about your own grade level or one particular grade level. What are some of the fundamental mathematical ideas or topics that build a foundation for later learning? How do those mathematical ideas or topics connect with learning in later grades?*

Learning Progressions and Examples

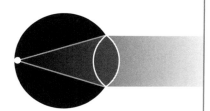

> The goal of a curriculum organized around Focal Points is that students' mathematical knowledge progresses and deepens over time.

The goal of a curriculum organized around Focal Points is that students' mathematical knowledge progresses and deepens over time. A focused curriculum emphasizes depth of understanding as well as connections among mathematical ideas. Students do not simply repeat previously learned topics or forget about topics they learned in previous grades. Instead, the identified Focal Points for a particular grade level build on the Focal Points from the previous grade, and at the same time lead the way for the Focal Points for the next grade. Students should practice and use previously learned concepts and skills but with an emphasis on building on from that knowledge.

An Example of the Learning Progression for Single-Digit Addition and Subtraction

> The identified Focal Points for a particular grade level build on the Focal Points from the previous grade, and at the same time lead the way for the Focal Points for the next grade.

As an example of a learning progression, let us take a look at how students' understanding of single-digit addition and subtraction progresses or develops over time. The "Addition and Subtraction Methods" figure that follows shows a sample progression of methods to solve basic addition and subtraction problems.

Initially, students often use a "count all" method using concrete objects, such as blocks, to represent the situation. To solve 8 + 6, a student first counts out and produces a set of eight blocks. Then the student counts out a second set of six blocks. Finally, the student puts all the blocks together and recounts all the blocks, saying, "1, 2, 3, 4, 5, 6, 7, 8, 9, 10, 11, 12, 13, 14." Students also count each set separately for subtraction. To solve 14 − 8, the student first counts out a set of fourteen blocks. Next, the student counts out and takes away eight of those blocks. Finally, the student counts the blocks that are left.

Later, students learn that they can abbreviate the process of counting both sets of numbers and can "count on" from the first addend (or the larger

Addition and Subtraction Methods

	8 + 6 = 14	14 − 8 = 6
Count all	a 1 2 3 4 5 6 7 8 1 2 3 4 5 6 b 1 2 3 4 5 6 7 8 9 10 11 12 13 14 c 9 10 11 12 13 14	a 1 2 3 4 5 6 7 8 9 10 11 12 13 14 b 1 2 3 4 5 6 7 8 1 2 3 4 5 6
Count on	8 Or use fingers to keep track of the six counted on. 9 10 11 12 13 14	To solve 14 − 8: I count on 8 + ? = 14. 9 10 11 12 13 14 I took away 8. 8 to 14 is 6, so 14 − 8 = 6.
Recompose Make a 10 (general): one addend breaks apart to make 10 with the other addend. Make a 10 (from 5s within each addend).	10 + 4 6 + 8 = 6 + 6 + 2 = 12 + 2 = 14	14 − 8: I make a 10 for 8 + ? = 14. 8 + 2 + 4 6 8 + 6 = 14
Doubles ± n		

addend). To solve 8 + 6, the child starts with 8 and then counts on 6 more, saying, "9, 10, 11, 12, 13, 14." As in the "count all" method, the student may still use concrete objects, such as blocks, to keep track of the six counted on or use his or her fingers. The counting-on method also works for subtraction when students learn to think of subtraction as the inverse of addition. To solve 14 – 8, a student first rethinks or rewrites this problem as "eight plus what equals fourteen" or "8 + ? = 14." Then the student counts on from 8 to 14, keeping track, often on his or her fingers, of how many were counted on to get to 14 ("9, 10, 11, 12, 13, 14, which is 6").

As students continue to progress in their learning of addition and subtraction, they may use more sophisticated strategies, such as decomposing and composing numbers to make 10 or using a particular known fact to derive a new fact. In the "make a 10" method, one addend is broken apart to "make 10" with the other addend. To solve 8 + 6 using this strategy, the 6 is broken apart into 2 + 4 so that the 8 and 2 can be then be combined to make 10, and now the problem is thought of as 10 + 4 = 14 [8 + 6 = 8 + 2 + 4 = 10 + 4]. The make-a-10 method can be used similarly for subtraction if the student first thinks of the related addition fact and then solves for the missing addend by completing the 10 and then adding on more to get to the final sum. To solve 14 – 8, a student first thinks of the related addition fact 8 + ? = 14. Next, the student makes 10 by thinking, "Eight plus 2 equals 10, and to get 14 I need to add 4 more, so adding the 2 and 4 together gives me 8 + 6 = 14."

Students can gain facility in the make-a-10 method for addition and subtraction by using a ten-frame and physically moving chips into the ten-frame to complete the 10. For example, to solve 8 + 6, the student places eight chips in the ten-frame. Then, he or she adds two of the chips from the second addend to the ten-frame to complete the 10, changing the problem to 10 + 4 = 14. In addition to using a ten-frame to practice the make-a-10 method, students can also make their own drawings to show this method, as well as use other methods, such as circling five from each addend to make a 10.

"Using doubles" is another strategy students might use. For example, to solve 6 + 8, a student could think of the double 6 + 6 = 12. Since 6 + 6 = 12, 6 + 7 is one more than that and 6 + 8 is two more than that, or 14. Or, a student could solve this same problem by thinking of the double 8 + 8 = 16, so 6 + 8 is two less than that, or 14.

DEVELOPMENT-OF-GEOMETRIC-THINKING TASK: *How does geometric thinking develop as students progress from prekindergarten through grade 2? What are other core topics in prekindergarten–grade 2, and how do those topics develop over time? NCTM's* **Curriculum Focal Points for Prekindergarten through Grade 8 Mathematics** *(2006) and the supporting grade-level books, NCTM's Navigations Series books, and your own curriculum documents are good references to use in this exercise.*

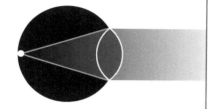

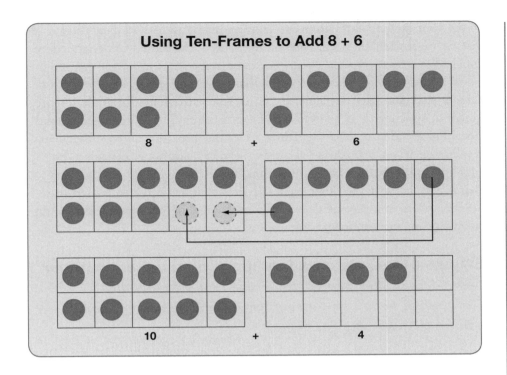

Using Ten-Frames to Add 8 + 6

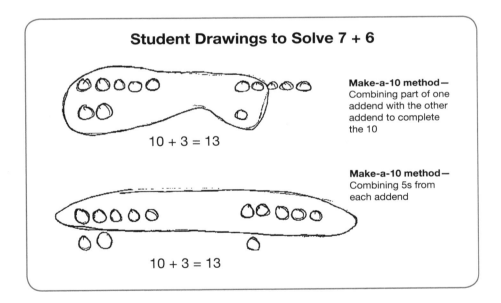

Student Drawings to Solve 7 + 6

10 + 3 = 13

Make-a-10 method— Combining part of one addend with the other addend to complete the 10

Make-a-10 method— Combining 5s from each addend

10 + 3 = 13

Focusing the Curriculum You Teach

Now that you have taken some time to think about learning progressions and how students' knowledge can grow and deepen over time, the next step is to look at your curriculum and begin to organize it into more coherent instruction at each grade level. This task may seem daunting, but the intent is

A sample state curriculum for grade 1 is provided in Appendix E as an example of a curriculum that is organized around Focal Points.

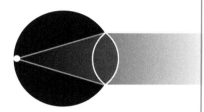

to use your existing curriculum as a starting point. States and districts may revise future curriculum documents on the basis of the framework provided by NCTM's *Curriculum Focal Points;* however, in the short term, you can use the Focal Points to prioritize topics of emphasis listed at each grade level in your current state and local curricula. A sample state curriculum for grade 1 is provided in Appendix E as an example of a curriculum that is organized around Focal Points (identified as "Big Ideas"). Use the questions in the subsequent Evaluating-My-Curriculum Task to begin to evaluate your curriculum by highlighting focal areas and connections, as well as by identifying content that might be moved to other grades or areas that seem to be repeated year after year. You might want to use different colored highlighter markers to distinguish your focal areas and connections.

EVALUATING-MY-CURRICULUM TASK: *Using your own curriculum for prekindergarten, kindergarten, grade 1, and grade 2 and NCTM's Curriculum Focal Points (see Appendixes A, B, and C, and D), address the following questions:*

- *Do I think we currently have a focused mathematics curriculum in prekindergarten–grade 2? Why or Why not?*

- *What key ideas or learning progressions can be seen in our existing mathematics curriculum at each grade level? Do any essential ideas appear in NCTM's set of Focal Points that do not appear somewhere in our curriculum, and vice versa? If so, how do we address that discrepancy?*

- *Does our sequence of key ideas make sense mathematically? Does it connect logically with the mathematics in earlier and later grade levels and build from grade to grade without unnecessary repetition? If not, how can we change this sequencing?*

- *Can we tell from our own curriculum what topics will receive the most emphasis and how these topics are treated differently in prekindergarten, kindergarten, grade 1, and grade 2? How much time would you propose be spent on these areas of emphasis, and should that time be dispersed throughout the year or concentrated?*

- *What content areas or topics in our existing curriculum can we think of as "connections" with the identified key ideas? Can we better connect these areas with our key ideas or areas of emphasis instead of teaching them as separate topics?*

- *In general, what changes can be made to our curriculum, both overall and within the prekindergarten–grade 2 grade band, to make it more focused?*

- *Do our current materials and textbooks support teaching to the depth of understanding required for students' knowledge to grow and deepen over time? What supplemental materials might be used to support this goal?*

- *What concerns do I have about the idea of a focused mathematics curriculum in prekindergarten–grade 2?*

Sample Responses to "Questions to Reflect On"

What are some of the major learning progressions that occur in prekindergarten–grade2?

The major learning progressions in prekindergarten–grade 2 relate to the content areas of Number and Operations, Geometry, and Measurement (see Appendixes A, B, C, and D). Related to the Number and Operations Standard, developing understanding of whole numbers and place value is a major focus in the prekindergarten–grade 2 curriculum. In prekindergarten, the development of whole-number concepts begins with being able to count small groups of objects, such as six blocks, and assigning the last counted number to that set to tell how many objects are in the set. Children also begin to recognize the number of objects in very small groups, such as three cookies, without counting. During kindergarten, students should be able to count up to 20 objects in a row and are starting to learn place-value concepts by counting up to 100 using the repeating pattern of the numbers 1–9 combined with the appropriate decade (i.e., thirty, thirty-one, thirty-two, thirty-three, thirty-four, thirty-five, thirty-six, thirty-seven, thirty-eight, thirty-nine, forty, forty-one, forty-two, and so on). These ideas progress to place-value concepts and grouping by tens and ones in grade 1 and by hundreds, tens, and ones in grade 2.

Another major focus in the prekindergarten–grade 2 curriculum related to the Number and Operations Standard is comparing whole numbers and adding and subtracting whole numbers. In prekindergarten and kindergarten, students compare sets to determine which group has the larger or smaller number of objects. They might match two sets up by lining them up in one-to-one correspondence and determine that the larger set has leftover objects that do not match up with the other set, or they might count each set out and determine the larger set as the one with the number that is farther along in the number-word list. In grade 1 and grade 2, these ideas progress to using place value and comparing the digits in the higher place-value positions to determine the larger number.

In prekindergarten and kindergarten, students solve simple addition and subtraction problems by modeling the situations with concrete objects or fingers and counting. The concept of joining sets of objects, the basic situation in addition problems, comes naturally for most young children. Initially they think of subtraction as taking away objects from a set. Later on, as they come to understand relationships between addition and subtraction, they can use the subtraction operation in other situations, such as comparing two quantities to determine how much more one quantity is than another (e.g., "I have 7 blocks. You have 3 blocks. How many more blocks do I have than you have?") or finding an unknown addend (e.g., "Kate had 2 crackers. Marcus gave her some more and now she has 6 crackers. How many crackers did Marcus give her?"). Students should be presented with many different types of addition and subtraction situations and should learn subtraction alongside addition so that they understand the relationship between these two operations. In grade 1, students develop understanding of whole numbers between 10 and 100 in terms of groups of tens and ones and use this knowledge to begin to solve two-digit addition and subtraction problems. In grade 2, students should develop fluency with efficient procedures for multidigit addition and subtraction problems.

Alongside number and operations, concepts in geometry and measurement are focused on and developed during the prekindergarten–grade 2 years. With respect to geometry, students begin to identify and describe two-and three-dimensional shapes in prekindergarten and kindergarten. Their learning progresses from being able to identify simple shapes, such as circles and squares, to recognizing different classes of shapes, such as a variety of triangles and rectangles, as well as identifying and describing other two-dimensional shapes, such as regular hexagons, and three-dimensional shapes, such as spheres, cubes, and cylinders. In grades 1 and 2, students are beginning to focus on properties of shapes and informally analyzing shapes. In grade 1, students compose and decompose plane and solid figures, such as put two congruent isosceles triangles together to make a rhombus or put two square blocks together to make a rectangular block. In the process of composing and decomposing shapes, students experiment with rotating and flipping the shapes and become more skilled at recognizing them from different perspectives and orientations, describing their geometric attributes and properties, and determining how shapes are alike and different. In grade 2, composing and decomposing shapes continues as a connection that is building a foundation for measurement ideas, such as area, fractions, and proportions. Students in prekindergarten–grade 2 typically are at level 0 (visualization) in the van Hiele hierarchy of the development of geometric thinking. At this level, appearance is dominant and students often group shapes together because they appear to look alike. For example, a square is a square "because it looks like a square." To a student at this level of thinking, a square that is rotated and not in the traditional orientation might be called a "diamond" and not a square. As students move to level 1 (analysis) in the van Hiele hierarchy, they judge a figure more by its properties than solely what it "looks like." The goal is to support students as they move to level 1 of the van Hiele hierarchy (NCTM 2001).

Measurement concepts begin early on for young children as they informally begin to identify measurable attributes and make comparisons. For example, when presented with two glasses to drink from, a child might say, "I want the big glass." Children in prekindergarten use measurement vocabulary, such as *long* and *short* and *heavy* and *light,* and work on the more difficult comparative terms *longer* and *shorter* or *heavier* and *lighter.* In kindergarten, students progress to comparing and ordering several objects by a measurable attribute, for example, lining up toys from shortest to longest. Students in kindergarten also compare the measurement attributes of two objects by using a third object, for instance, comparing the heights of individual students by using a length of string. Measurement concepts continue as a connection in grade 1 as students continue to solve problems involving measurements and data. In grade 2, students focus on linear measurement and progress in their understanding of core ideas in measurement, such as partitioning (the mental activity of slicing the length of an object into equal-sized units), unit iteration (repeatedly placing a smaller object end-to-end along the length of a larger object), and transitivity (e.g., if object A is longer than object B and object B is longer than object C, then object A is longer than object C).

Appendix F of this book links specific activities from NCTM's Navigations Series with the Focal Points identified at each grade level. Grade-level books related to the Focal Points will also be produced for prekindergarten, kindergarten, grade1, and grade 2 and will serve as important resources for teachers, as well.

> Appendix F of this book links specific activities from NCTM's Navigations Series with the Focal Points identified at each grade level.

How are basic facts and algorithms addressed in a focused curriculum?

Many of the Focal Points in prekindergarten–grade 2 relate to the content strand of Number and Operations, so needless to say, basic facts and fluent use of algorithms (or procedures) to solve computational problems are important. However, facts and procedures must be learned with understanding. Instruction in basic facts should emphasize thinking strategies, and students should first develop understanding of the meanings of addition and subtraction before being expected to quickly recall facts. Students should develop fluency in efficient procedures for multidigit addition and subtraction problems, including standard algorithms for each of those operations; however, these skills should always be developed alongside understanding. To gain facility in using these procedures, students must focus on why the procedures work by using place-value concepts and properties of operations. For example, students begin to make more sense of the standard algorithm for subtracting multidigit numbers when regrouping is necessary after they have developed an understanding of multidigit numbers in terms of place value and have had practice composing and decomposing such numbers. For example, the standard written algorithm used to solve 35 − 17 will make more sense to students if they understand that the number 35 originally represented by 3 tens and 5 ones can also be represented as 2 tens and 15 ones. Students can act out the steps of the standard algorithm by using base-ten blocks or by creating drawings of tens and ones as shown in the subsequent figure. By using base-ten blocks or making drawings as they solve the problem, students can connect the physical process of decomposing numbers with the numerical steps in the algorithm. Students might use strategies other than the standard algorithm to think about and solve the problem 35 − 17. For example, with a "counting up" strategy, a student might think, "I added up from 17 to get to 20. That's 3. Then from 20 to 35 is another 15. Fifteen

Standard Subtraction Algorithm
Solved with Drawings of Tens and Ones

Step 1: Draw 35 with 10-sticks and ones and look to see what I can subtract.

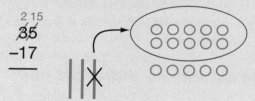

Step 2: I need to take away 7 ones, but I only have 5 ones, so I need to open up a 10 to make 10 ones.

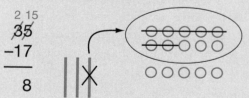

Step 3: Now I take 7 ones from 15 ones, which leaves 8 ones. I can also think 7 up to 10 is 3 and 5 more is 8.

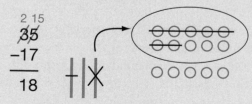

Step 4: Now I subtract my 10s.

plus 3 is 18, so 35 – 17 = 18." Another student might think about the same problem in this way: "I changed the 35 to 37 and first solved 37 – 17, which is 20. Then I have to subtract the 2 I added, which gives me 18." Such strategies as these, built on decomposing and recomposing numbers, allow students to become flexible in their thinking and solve problems mentally in addition to using and understanding the standard paper-and-pencil algorithm.

Instruction to Support a Focused Curriculum

Questions to Reflect On

- **What characterizes instruction that supports depth of understanding and connections among mathematical ideas?**
- **How can questioning be used to support the development of depth of understanding and connections in a focused curriculum?**
- **What is the role of practice in a focused curriculum?**
- **What impact does instruction that supports a focused curriculum have on time management?**

Although NCTM's Curriculum Focal Points can help prioritize and organize mathematics content, teachers and the instruction they provide are crucial to using Focal Points to improve students' learning. Focusing mathematics instruction on a few central ideas at each grade requires skilled teachers who know the content well and can connect mathematical ideas and teach for depth of understanding.

The Use of the Process Standards

Teachers must incorporate the Process Standards of Problem Solving, Reasoning and Proof, Communication, Connections, and Representation as described in *Principles and Standards for School Mathematics* (NCTM 2000) into classroom instruction. Teachers should create a climate that supports mathematical thinking and communication. In this kind of classroom, students are accustomed to reasoning about a mathematical problem and justifying or explaining their results, representing mathematical ideas in multiple ways, and building new knowledge, as well as applying knowledge through problem solving. Brief descriptions of the Process Standards can be found in the table that follows. More detailed descriptions can be found in *Principles and Standards for School Mathematics* (NCTM 2000).

Effective mathematics teaching requires understanding what students know and need to learn and then challenging and supporting them to learn it well.

—The Teaching Principle, *Principles and Standards for School Mathematics*

Focusing mathematics instruction on a few central ideas at each grade requires skilled teachers who know the content well and can connect mathematical ideas and teach for depth of understanding.

The NCTM Process Standards

Problem Solving. Through problem solving, students can not only apply the knowledge and skills they have acquired but can also learn new mathematical content. Problem solving is not a specific skill to be taught, but should permeate all aspects of learning. Teachers should make an effort to choose "good" problems—ones that invite exploration of an important mathematical concept and allow students the chance to solidify and extend their knowledge. For example, suppose a first-grade class is working on learning the basic addition facts. Instead of simply giving the students a list of addition problems to solve, such as 3 + 2, the teacher could ask the students to build as many different towers of five cubes using only two different colors of cubes (see figure below). Such an activity not only helps students understand and learn basic addition facts but also explores the commutative property as well as connections to other areas, such as patterns. A subsequent activity could involve building towers of ten cubes using only two different colors. The instructional strategies used in the classroom should also promote collaborative problem solving. Students' learning of mathematics is enhanced in a learning environment that is a community of people collaborating to make sense of mathematical ideas (Hiebert et al. 1997).

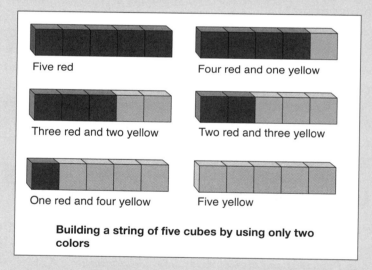

Five red

Four red and one yellow

Three red and two yellow

Two red and three yellow

One red and four yellow

Five yellow

Building a string of five cubes by using only two colors

Reasoning and Proof. For students to learn mathematics with understanding, it must make sense to them. Teachers can help students make sense of the mathematics they are learning by encouraging them to always explain and justify their solutions and strategies, as well as to evaluate other students' ideas. Questions such as "Why?" and "How do you know?" should be a regular part of classroom discussions. The teacher should respond in ways that focus on thinking and reasoning rather than only on getting the correct answer. Incorrect answers should not simply be judged wrong. Instead, teachers can help students identify the parts of their thinking that may be correct, often leading to new ideas and solutions that are correct.

Communication. Reasoning and proof go hand in hand with the process of communication. Students should have plenty of opportunities and support for speaking, writing, reading, and listening in the mathematics classroom. Communicating one's ideas orally and in writing helps solidify and refine learning. Listening to others' explanations can also sharpen learning by providing multiple ways to think about a problem. The teacher plays an important role in developing students' communication skills by modeling effective oral and written communication of mathematical ideas as well as giving students regular opportunities to communicate mathematically. Precise mathematical vocabulary and definitions are important, and teachers need to help students articulate these ideas and ensure that students understand these ideas during class discussions.

Connections. As students move through the grades, they should be presented with new mathematical content. Students' abilities to understand these new ideas depend greatly on connecting the new ideas with previously learned ideas. Mathematics is an integrated field of study and should be presented in this way instead of as a set of disconnected and isolated concepts and skills. Instruction should emphasize the interconnectedness of mathematical ideas both within and across grade levels and should be presented in a variety of contexts.

Representation. Mathematical ideas can be represented in a variety of ways: pictures, concrete materials, tables, graphs, numerical and alphabetical symbols, spreadsheet displays, and so on. Such representations should be an essential part of learning and doing mathematics and should serve as a tool for thinking about and solving problems. Teachers should model representing mathematical ideas in a variety of ways and discuss why some representations are more effective than others in particular situations.

Facilitating Classroom Discourse

The Process Standards, especially the Communication Standard and the Reasoning and Proof Standard, are related to the discourse in the mathematics classroom. "The discourse of a classroom—the way of representing, thinking, talking, agreeing, and disagreeing—is central to what and how students learn mathematics" (NCTM 2007, p. 46). The teacher plays an important role in initiating and facilitating this discourse and can do so by—

- posing questions and tasks that elicit, engage, and challenge each student's thinking;

- listening carefully to students' ideas and deciding what to pursue in depth from among the ideas that students generate during a discussion;

- asking students to clarify and justify their ideas orally and in writing and by accepting a variety of presentation modes;

- deciding when and how to attach mathematical notation and language to students' ideas;

- encouraging and accepting the use of multiple representations;

- making available tools for exploration and analysis;

- deciding when to provide information, when to clarify an issue, when to model, when to lead, and when to let students wrestle with a difficulty; and

- monitoring students' participation in discussions and deciding when and how to encourage each student to participate. (NCTM 2007, p. 45)

The following classroom vignette depicts a kindergarten teacher facilitating a discussion about counting.

Kindergarten Vignette

Ms. Nakamura has done a lot of number work with her kindergarten class this year, and she is pleased with the results. Now, near the end of the year, the class has been investigating patterns in the number of various body parts in the classroom—how many noses or eyes, for example, are present among the children in the class.

Earlier that week, each child had made a nose out of clay. Ms. Nakamura opens the discussion by revisiting that project. She asks, "And how many noses did we make?"

Becky (points to her nostrils): Two of these.

Teacher:	But how many actual noses?
Anne:	Twenty-nine.
Teacher:	Why? Why were there twenty-nine noses?
Adam:	Because every kid in the class made one clay nose, and that is the same number as kids in the class.

Teacher (pointing to her nostrils): Now Becky just said—remember what these are called?

Children:	Nostrils!
Teacher:	So were there twenty-nine nostrils?
Pat:	No, there were more.

Gwen:	Fifty-eight! We had fifty-eight nostrils!
Teacher:	Why fifty-eight?
Gwen:	I counted.
Felice:	If we had thirty kids, we would be sixty. So it is fifty-nine 'cause it should be one less.
Teacher:	Can you explain that again?

The teacher probes Felice's answer even though her approach goes beyond what many of the children are trying to do at this point.

Felice:	It's fifty-nine because we don't have thirty kids, we have twenty-nine, so it is one less than sixty.
Teacher:	What does anyone else think?
Adam:	I think it is fifty-eight. Each kid has two nostrils. So if sixty would be for thirty kids, then it has to be two less: fifty-eight.

The teacher solicits other students' reactions instead of showing them the right answer. Her tone of voice and her questions show the students that she values their thinking.

Lawrence:	But Felice says thirty kids makes sixty …
Felice:	No! Adam makes sense. Fifty-eight.

The teacher moves on, asking, "What else do you think we have on our bodies that would be more than twenty-nine?"

The teacher's question challenges students to think it is open-ended; more than one right answer exists.

Graham:	More than twenty-nine fingers.
Teacher:	More than twenty-nine fingers? Why do you think so?
Graham:	Because each kid, we have ten fingers.
Ricky:	More than twenty-nine shoes.
Teacher:	More than twenty-nine shoes. And what are those shoes covering?
Ricky:	Your feet.
Sarah:	Ears.
Beth:	More than twenty-nine legs.

Ms. Nakamura tells the children, "You did some good thinking today!" The teacher chooses to comment on the children's thinking instead of their behavior.

Ms. Nakamura tells the children that they now are to work on a picture: "Choose some body part, and draw a picture of how many of those we have in our class and how you know that." She directs the children back to their tables, where she has laid out paper and cans of crayons.

Source: *Mathematics Teaching Today* (Martin 2007, pp. 48–50).

Most students in prekindergarten–grade 2 naturally share their ideas and thinking and are comfortable talking aloud as they solve problems. The teacher's role is to help sustain and advance these discussions, particularly with the intent of highlighting essential mathematical ideas. In the classroom example in the preceding vignette, the teacher's use of questioning and asking students to explain and justify their solutions invites many students to participate in the discussion. The dialogue clearly shows that the students in this classroom are accustomed to sharing their ideas and not relying on the teacher as the sole authority for solutions to problems. They are learning to be mathematical thinkers and to listen to and question others' approaches to solving problems, behaviors that help solidify their own mathematical knowledge.

The Use of Questioning to Focus Learning and Promote Connections

> A teacher's use of questioning plays a vital role in focusing learning on foundational mathematical ideas and promoting mathematical connections.

As described in the introduction and the "Focusing Curriculum" section of this guide, using Focal Points to organize instruction does not mean teaching less or more content, but instead means directing the majority of instruction at a smaller number of core areas with the goal of students' gaining a deeper mathematical understanding of those mathematical ideas and the connections among them. To teach for depth of understanding, teachers need to understand what their students are thinking and be able to support and extend that thinking. A teacher's use of questioning plays a vital role in focusing learning on foundational mathematical ideas and promoting mathematical connections. Such reasoning questions as "Why?" and "How do you know that?" posed during a lesson are great starters, but teachers also need to incorporate questioning techniques into their planning by thinking about specific questions to ask related to the particular topic being studied. When planning instruction, teachers must also anticipate the kinds of answers they might get from students in response to the questions posed.

Let us look at the following classroom example to show a teacher's use of questioning as well as students' questioning in a second-grade lesson that focuses on place-value concepts and multidigit addition.

Second-Grade Vignette

Teacher: Here's our first problem for today (points to a horizontal 76 + 58 written on the board). Who can give me a word problem for this? Doug?

Doug: There were 76 girls and 58 boys waiting for the buses. How many children are waiting?

Teacher: So we're all going to solve this in our own ways. Then three of the people at the board will explain their methods and how they relate to their drawings. [Pause as everyone solves, some helping others or explaining to others after they solve.] Juanita, can you please explain your method?

Juanita: I showed my totals separately. I added 70 and 50 to get 120. And then I added 8 and 6 to get 14. Then I needed to find out how much I had in all. So I added these two totals and I got 134 children waiting for the buses. Any questions? Sara.

Sara: Why did you add the 70 and 50 first?

Juanita: Because it is like reading—start over here and go this way [moving her hand across the number from left to right.] And it doesn't matter whether you add the tens or the ones first, you'll get the same totals and then the same final answer. Any more questions? OK, if not then it is Yeping's turn to explain.

Yeping: I started with the ones. I added 8 ones and 6 ones and got 14 ones, which is more than I can write in the ones place. So I made 10 ones to give to the tens place (points to drawing where he circled 10 ones), and I wrote this new 1 ten above the tens place. Then I added my tens. One ten and 7 tens is 8 tens (points to the top of the problem), and 5 more tens is 13 tens. Questions?

Dan: Why did you split up the 8 in your drawing to make 10 instead of starting with the 8 and taking 2 from the 6? That's easier for me.

Yeping: The 6 was first in the problem, and it is not that much harder for me to add 8 to 6. I can count on or make a 10 in my drawing either way. No more questions? OK, Sam.

Sam: I added the 6 ones to the 8 ones. I could see that I needed 2 more ones to make a 10 with the 8, so I circled 2 ones in the 6 to make 10. I didn't want to put the new 10 above the top number like Yeping did because that changes the problem, so I put mine down at the bottom, waiting on the line until I had added the 70 and the 50 to make 120. See [pointing to the left side of the drawing], the 70 just needed 3 more tens to make 1 hundred, and the 2 tens left in 50 makes 120. And my 1 more ten added in makes 130. Marisol?

Marisol: I really like how you put the new ten below. Because look how it is easier to add in the problem than in Yeping's way because you just add the two numbers you see: 7 tens and 5 tens, and then add the extra ten. Yeping had to add in his new ten to the 7 to make 8, which we can't see in the problem, and then add that to the 5 tens.

Saul: I like having the new ten down below because I forget to

	add it when it is above, like my brother taught me. And I can write the 14 as one four like usual. In my brother's way, I'd sometimes write the 1 below and the 4 above because I'd write the 1 first when writing 14. And look, you can see that it is fourteen because they're together.
Teacher:	So what is happening across all of these methods? What issue does everyone have to solve in how they write their method?
Ana:	We had too many ones to write them in the ones place. So everyone wrote that new ten they had to make from the ones in different places.
Teacher:	Yes, Juanita wrote it as the 1 in 14 (pointing to Juanita's problem) when she added the ones, Yeping wrote it above the tens column (pointing at the 1 new ten above), and Sam wrote it down here below the problem (pointing) in the tens column waiting to add it. Steve?
Steve:	And everyone just wrote the new 1 hundred in the next column because there weren't any other hundreds in the numbers.
Teacher:	Yes, when we get to problems with some hundreds, we'll have to do something like these methods with the hundreds also. Tomorrow we'll do some more problems like this and discuss the advantages and disadvantages of each method of writing the new 1 ten some more. I especially want you to think about Sam's comment—does writing the new 1 ten above change the problem? Now who wants to say something about how these drawings help us see how to find the single-digit totals if we don't just know them? Asha?
Asha:	We can see the make-a-ten method in Sam's drawing because the 8 shows how many we need to make ten and then there are four left in six to make ten and four. But I can do that in my head without the drawing, but last year I needed the drawing.
Teacher:	Yes, Sam made ten by combing 2 of the ones from the 6 with the 8, and then he was left with 4 ones.
Julie:	I think how Juanita did it with the ones is cool. She made a ten with the fives in six and eight, and it looks like a big ten-stick with 10 ones on it. So for some numbers you can think of the numbers over five and add those to make the ones in the teen number.
Teacher:	Great, that's another strategy—combine 5 ones from each of the single-digit numbers you are adding to make ten, and then add the ones that are left from each number.

Yolanda:	Yeping did it both ways. For the ten-sticks he put together two groups of 5 tens to make 10 tens. But for the ones he took 4 from the 8 to make a 10 with the 6.
Yeping:	Yes, I only use both fives when one number is a 5. I do it in my head then because it is 1 ten and the ones are the number over five in the other number, here it is two.
Teacher:	Two what?
Yeping:	Two tens, so 1 hundred and 2 tens. But in my problem I added the 1 ten first to make 8 tens. So I guess I'd have to write the new 10 below like Sam to add 7 and 5 the way I did in my drawing.
Teacher:	Many of you now are not needing the drawings to know what to do with your new ten or new hundred or to add the numbers. So you don't need to make a drawing when you solve, but it helps to make one when you are explaining your method up at the board. Great job solving, explaining, and helping each other!

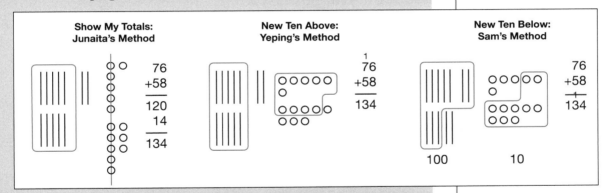

Source: Videotaped transcriptions, *Children's Math Worlds Research Project*, Karen C. Fuson, Northwestern University

This is an example of a teacher's questioning to steer the discussion to focus on essential ideas, particularly the idea of regrouping ones and tens in solving multidigit addition problems. We also observe students' use of questions for the purpose of understanding one another's solution methods. As in the previous vignette, the exchange clearly shows that the students in this classroom are accustomed to sharing their own ideas as well as listening to other's ideas. With appropriate modeling by the teacher and repeated opportunities for practice, young children are capable of achieving this level of student-to-student discourse. Once students are used to this type of interaction, it can be a powerful learning tool as students learn from one another and solidify their knowledge through these discussions. The teacher plays an important role in asking questions to guide the conversation and challenge students' thinking, but the teacher also lets students think about and discover important concepts on their own.

Students must learn mathematics with understanding, actively building new knowledge from experience and prior knowledge.

—The Learning Principle, *Principles and Standards for School Mathematics*

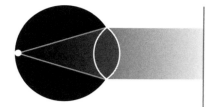

QUESTIONING TASK: *Below are a few different classroom assignments that might be given to students in prekindergarten–grade 2. Identify any essential ideas that these activities address. Generate a list of questions that you might ask to focus students' attention on these important ideas and to forge mathematical connections.*

Student Assignment 1

Lisa is making bracelets. She has already made 8 bracelets. She needs to make 12 so she can give one to each of her cousins. How many more bracelets does she need to make? Show how you solved this problem. Use pictures, numbers, and words.

Source: *Mathematics Assessment Sampler, Prekindergarten–Grade 2* (Huinker 2006, p. 24).

Student Assignment 2

Robin found some bugs. She gave 5 to her brother and kept 8 to show at school. How many bugs did Robin find? Show how you solved this problem. Use pictures, numbers, and words.

Student Assignment 3

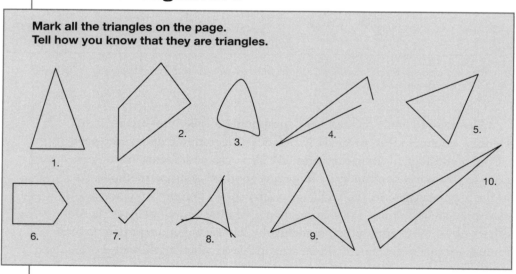

Mark all the triangles on the page.
Tell how you know that they are triangles.

Source: *Mathematics Assessment Sampler, Prekindergarten–Grade 2* (Huinker 2006, p. 96).

Student Assignment 4

Source: *Mathematics Assessment: A Practical Handbook for Grades K–2* (Glanfield, Bush, and Stenmark 2003, p. 146).

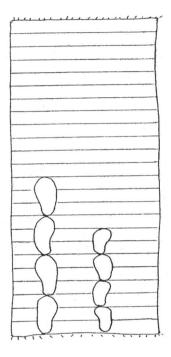

Look at the foot steps on the rug.
Dad measures the rug by counting his steps.
Alisha measures the rug by counting her steps.

Show how you would figure out how many of Dad's steps fit on the rug.

Show how you would figure out how many of Alisha's steps fit on the rug.

CORRECTING-STUDENT-ERROR TASK: *You notice that many of your students are forgetting to regroup when using the traditional subtraction algorithm. See example below. What questioning or other techniques would you use to help the student correct his or her thinking?*

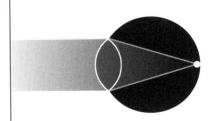

$$\begin{array}{r} 174 \\ -\ 89 \\ \hline 115 \end{array}$$

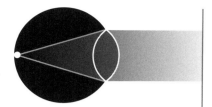

DEVELOPING-DEPTH-OF-UNDERSTANDING TASK: *Choose a Focal Point for prekindergarten, kindergarten, grade 1, or grade 2. What kinds of activities might you do with your class to help students acquire depth of understanding?*

Sample Responses to "Questions to Reflect On"

What is the role of practice in a focused curriculum?

Practice of mathematical skills is necessary. For example, practice can help students become more confident and competent in using a computational procedure. Practice can also help commit facts to long-term memory, thereby freeing up working memory for more complex problems (National Mathematics Advisory Panel 2007, slides 6–7). However, if students are mimicking a procedure without understanding the procedure and why it works, they often make mistakes and the practice can solidify errors. For example, students need to relate their understanding of place-value concepts and grouping in tens and ones to their steps in multidigit subtraction. Showing these relationships for each step by using a mathematical drawing or base-ten blocks can help build understanding that can later be drawn on to check answers or troubleshoot errors. Practice in a focused curriculum may also help connect previously learned material with the new Focal Point areas. For example, when students begin to focus on multidigit multiplication in grade 4, they will also be practicing or reinforcing their skills in multidigit addition learned in grade 2.

What impact does instruction that supports a focused curriculum have on time management?

Probably the phrase that is heard most from teachers (and rightly so) is "I don't have enough time...," whether it is in reference to planning, teaching, or assessing. However, the Focal Points model is designed to have a positive impact on teachers' time. Reorganizing the curriculum into focus areas will result in less repetition and reteaching and more time for rigorous, in-depth study of important mathematics at each grade level. An important consideration for teachers to think about is *quality of time* and how they might use their time differently both in planning and during instruction. Instead of teaching "a skill a day," teachers need to have a more holistic plan for instruction. Teachers might think about "What essential understandings and connections do I want my students to have?" and "What sequence of lessons will I use to promote these understandings and connections?" as they plan for instruction. Teachers need to spend time thinking carefully about the examples and problems they will choose to support a mathematical concept and the questions they will ask to focus students' thinking, as well as ways to address anticipated responses. In the end, however, this time spent up front by teachers in planning should pay off both during instruction and in assessment as students connect mathematical ideas and learn mathematics with a greater depth of understanding.

Teachers' Mathematical Knowledge and Professional Development

Questions to Reflect On

- **What special knowledge of mathematics is needed by teachers to teach a focused curriculum?**
- **How can a culture of mathematics learning that supports teaching a focused curriculum be created?**
- **How can in-school and districtwide professional development be changed to improve teachers' mathematical knowledge?**

Mathematical Knowledge Needed by Teachers

Besides knowing students and instructional practices to support learning, teachers need a strong knowledge of the mathematics content themselves. However, what specific knowledge of mathematics is needed to teach mathematics, especially at the elementary school level? Shulman introduced the term *pedagogical content knowledge,* which he claimed went beyond a knowledge of subject matter to the subject-matter knowledge needed for teaching (Shulman 1986). Such knowledge includes a variety of special mathematics teaching skills, for example—

- knowing which concepts are typically difficult for students and how to address those difficulties;
- being able to select and model effective representations for mathematical ideas;
- selecting good problems;
- examining students' work and being able to pinpoint and analyze sources of errors;
- being flexible in thinking about alternative ways to solve a problem as described by students;

- assessing students so as to make important instructional decisions related to the content, such as when to provide additional instruction or when to move on; and

- deciding which student-generated ideas to call attention to during class discussions.

All these teaching tasks require a special kind of mathematical knowledge that is more than just knowing the mathematics for oneself.

Another resource about the knowledge needed for teaching is Liping Ma's book *Knowing and Teaching Elementary Mathematics* (Ma 1999). In her study, Ma compared Chinese and U.S. elementary school teachers' mathematical knowledge. Even having only eleven to twelve years of formal schooling versus the sixteen to eighteen years of most U.S. teachers, most of the Chinese teachers had a solid knowledge of the mathematics they taught, and some had what she called a "profound understanding of fundamental mathematics." This foundation included not only the ability to explain the mathematics taught and the ability to make up problems to illustrate what needs to be learned but also having a broader view of elementary school mathematics, which involves knowing what students should know before teaching a topic and knowing how the topic fits into later mathematical learning. It is developed only after years of teaching, but we need to prepare our teachers with enough knowledge to enable them to use their knowledge of mathematics, of students, and of teaching students to grow through the years as some of the Chinese teachers did. Most of the Chinese teachers Ma interviewed had a connected and coherent knowledge of core mathematical ideas similar to what NCTM's Curriculum Focal Points advocate.

Ma's work also contradicts the myth that "elementary mathematics is 'basic,' superficial, and commonly understood" (p. 146). Instead, elementary school mathematics can be quite intense and demanding, and it lays the important groundwork on which all future mathematics learning is based. Elementary school teachers must themselves possess a strong mathematical understanding of the underpinnings of elementary mathematics if they are to impart this wisdom to their students.

The following classroom scenario was presented in *Knowing and Teaching Elementary Mathematics* (Ma 1999). Discuss how you would address teaching this topic in your own classroom.

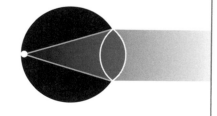

SUBTRACTION-WITH-REGROUPING TASK: *Look at these problems:*

$$\begin{array}{r} 52 \\ -\ 25 \\ \hline \end{array} \qquad \begin{array}{r} 91 \\ -\ 79 \\ \hline \end{array}$$

How would you approach these problems if you were teaching second grade? What would you say pupils would need to understand or be able to do before they could start learning subtraction with regrouping?

School Culture and Professional Development

Teaching a more focused curriculum at each grade level will be a major shift for most teachers and schools. Important considerations to remember are that these efforts will take time, and that collaboration among all parties involved is essential. A school culture must be developed that supports open discussions among teachers, instructional leaders, and administrators about how this outcome can be realized and what short- and long-term changes need to be made to implement the changes. Professional development must also include more emphasis on teachers' mathematical knowledge as well as pedagogical knowledge of how to teach that content in ways that promote a deeper understanding of the important mathematical ideas and connections. The identified Focal Points and Connections at each grade level could be the bases for designing professional development activities to improve teachers' mathematical knowledge.

PROFESSIONAL-DEVELOPMENT-PLAN TASK: *Work with other teachers in your grade or across grades to develop a professional development plan that will support teaching a focused curriculum. Identify short- and long-term goals.*

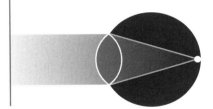

Assessment

Questions to Reflect On

- **How do we measure the depth of understanding that a focused curriculum is meant to impart?**
- **How do we measure the sophistication of students' strategies used to solve problems or their fluency with numbers?**
- **What is the role of classroom assessments in a focused curriculum?**
- **What role do state assessments play in a focused curriculum? In what ways might state assessments be changed to better promote a focused curriculum?**

Assessment should support the learning of important mathematics and furnish useful information to both teachers and students.

–Principles and Standards for School Mathematics

> Assessments must also measure the level or depth of students' understanding rather than simply ascertain whether the correct answer was given.

Focusing Assessment

How does having a more focused curriculum affect assessments? Overall, if the curriculum is more focused on core areas at each grade level, then in turn, assessments should also be more focused and should attempt to monitor and measure students' progress through these core areas. In addition, if the main goal of a focused curriculum is to develop depth of understanding, assessments must also measure the level or depth of students' understanding rather than simply ascertain whether the correct answer was given. Consider the grade 1 Focal Point of "Developing understandings of addition and subtraction and strategies for basic addition facts and related subtraction facts." Although quick recall of these facts is the ultimate goal and is a Focal Point the following year in grade 2, assessing students on their basic facts is much more than giving them a list of basic addition and subtraction problems to solve. The grade 1 Focal Point related to basic addition and subtract facts includes many components of developing understanding, such as understanding the meanings of addition and subtraction and being able to determine the addition or subtraction problem to solve when given a specific scenario, understanding the connections between counting and the operations of addition and subtraction (e.g., adding two is the same as "counting on" two), using the commutative and associative properties to develop strategies to add whole numbers (e.g., "making tens"), and recognizing the mathematical relationship between addition and subtraction (e.g., $5 - 2 = 3$ because $3 + 2 = 5$).

Measuring the Depth of Understanding

Open-ended questioning and tasks often yield more insight into students' understanding and thinking than multiple-choice problems or ones for which an answer—without justification or reasoning—is expected. Such open-ended problems usually ask students to explain their thinking, show their work, or otherwise provide more information than just an answer. Even problems that clearly have only one correct answer can be made more open-ended by asking students to justify or explain their answers. Sometimes a student will give the correct answer but provide reasoning that may reveal misconceptions and lack of true understanding. Similarly, a student may give a wrong answer because of a procedural or computational error but still understand the concept.

In the prekindergarten–grade 2 years, children often have more knowledge than they are able to express in writing. Their written work may offer only a piece of what they know and think, so teachers also need to rely on observations and engage students in conversations to assess their understanding. Consider the following students' explanations in response to a basic subtraction problem:

"How would you find the answer to 9 – 5?"

Student #1: "The answer is 9. When I take away the 5 [covers it up with hand], I get 9."

Student #2: Student puts 9 blocks on the table and counts back: "9, 8, 7, 6, 5—5 is the answer."

Student #3: Student puts 9 blocks on the table and removes 5. "Four are left."

Student #4: "The answer is 5." Student holds up fingers and counts on from five: "5, 6, 7, 8, 9."

Source: *Mathematics Assessment; A Practical Handbook for Grades K–2* (Glanfield, Bush, and Stenmark 2003).

In this example, the teacher can gain insight into each student's thinking by asking him or her to explain out loud how he or she would arrive at the answer. The third student seems to understand the "taking away" meaning for subtraction. The first student takes a literal approach to the problem and does not seem to understand the meaning of subtraction. The second student uses a counting-back method but starts with the number 9 instead of 8 (a common error when counting back). Similarly, the fourth student uses a counting-on method, but starts with the number 5 instead of 6. To learn more, the teacher might ask each of these students to show how he or she would solve other basic subtraction problems. Is the same mistake happening each time, or was it a one-time error? The teacher should also engage each student in additional conversation to learn whether the student understands the procedure he or she is using. Is the student connecting the procedure with the meaning of subtraction, or is the student rotely using a procedure without any understanding?

SAMPLE-STUDENT-WORK TASK: *Evaluate the sample student work in Appendix G for depth of understanding. What follow-up questions might you ask the students to get a more complete picture of their reasoning and understanding?*

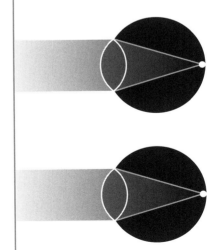

MEASURING-DEPTH-OF-UNDERSTANDING TASK: *What might an assessment that tries to measure the depth and complexity of one of the Focal Points for prekindergarten, kindergarten, grade 1, or grade 2 look like? Develop a sample assessment task that you might give to students related to that focal point.*

Classroom Assessment versus Large-Scale Assessment

Daily classroom assessment is crucial to a focused curriculum and the goal of having students' knowledge deepen over time. Teachers gather assessment information from a variety of sources, such as classroom observations, students' responses to questions and classroom discussions, daily classroom work, homework, performance tasks, students' journals, portfolios of sample work, quizzes, and tests. The kinds of classroom assessments will not likely change, but the Focal Points and Connections identified for a particular grade should be used to help teachers narrow in on what they want to assess. Those Focal Points should be at the forefront of a teacher's mind when planning instruction and assessments. Teachers must also analyze their students' level of understanding and fluency or sophistication in solving problems, then plan their instruction with the goal of advancing students' understanding.

Although large-scale assessments, such as state tests, can provide some useful data, these tests do not always furnish an accurate view of students' depth of understanding. Often, such tests are written to measure a very specific skill, for example, the ability to add two two-digit numbers. In addition, such tests usually attempt to measure a broad range of topics, and teachers' attempts to give coverage to all of them results in not having enough time to develop students' depth of understanding. As states change their curricula to be more focused at each grade level, state assessments should change as well. In the short term, teachers will have to balance the requirements of their state tests with organizing their instruction to promote important areas of emphasis and a greater depth of understanding.

Since mandated state testing for mathematics does not usually occur below grade 3, teachers in prekindergarten–grade 2 have an important responsibility to help lay the groundwork for the mathematics learning that takes place in later grades. The use of time for instruction and assessment in these early grades will affect the learning and assessment of students in grades 3–5 and beyond.

> The Focal Points and Connections identified for a particular grade should be used to help teachers narrow in on what they want to assess.

Concluding Thoughts

NCTM's *Curriculum Focal Points for Prekindergarten through Grade 8 Mathematics: A Quest for Coherence* was written as a framework to guide states and school districts as they design and organize the next revisions of their expectations, standards, curricula, and assessment programs. The goal of this guide is to expand on those ideas and provide a professional development tool to help individual teachers and groups of teachers begin to think about what a focused curriculum means and how they might begin to build some focus into their existing curriculum. By focusing more intensely on fewer topics at each grade level, students should gain a deeper understanding of mathematical ideas that will continue to grow and become more sophisticated as they move through the grades. As you work through your own professional development plan to build focus into your curriculum and teaching over the year, take time to revisit the "Questions to Reflect On" at the beginning of each section, as well as some of the professional development tasks presented throughout this guide. In what ways has your instruction become more focused? What changes have you seen in the level of understanding of your students? What additional goals do you have for bringing focus to your curriculum and instruction?

Appendix A

Curriculum Focal Points and Connections for Prekindergarten

The set of three curriculum focal points and related connections for mathematics in prekindergarten follow. These topics are the recommended content emphases for this grade level. It is essential that these focal points be addressed in contexts that promote problem solving, reasoning, communication, making connections, and designing and analyzing representations.

Prekindergarten Curriculum Focal Points	Connections to the Focal Points
Number and Operations: Developing an understanding of whole numbers, including concepts of correspondence, counting, cardinality, and comparison Children develop an understanding of the meanings of whole numbers and recognize the number of objects in small groups without counting and by counting—the first and most basic mathematical algorithm. They understand that number words refer to quantity. They use one-to-one correspondence to solve problems by matching sets and comparing number amounts and in counting objects to 10 and beyond. They understand that the last word that they state in counting tells "how many," they count to determine number amounts and compare quantities (using language such as "more than" and "less than"), and they order sets by the number of objects in them. **Geometry: Identifying shapes and describing spatial relationships** Children develop spatial reasoning by working from two perspectives on space as they examine the shapes of objects and inspect their relative positions. They find shapes in their environments and describe them in their own words. They build pictures and designs by combining two- and three-dimensional shapes, and they solve such problems as deciding which piece will fit into a space in a puzzle. They discuss the relative positions of objects with vocabulary such as "above," "below," and "next to." **Measurement: Identifying measurable attributes and comparing objects by using these attributes** Children identify objects as "the same" or "different," and then "more" or "less," on the basis of attributes that they can measure. They identify measurable attributes such as length and weight and solve problems by making direct comparisons of objects on the basis of those attributes.	*Data Analysis:* Children learn the foundations of data analysis by using objects' attributes that they have identified in relation to geometry and measurement (e.g., size, quantity, orientation, number of sides or vertices, color) for various purposes, such as describing, sorting, or comparing. For example, children sort geometric figures by shape, compare objects by weight ("heavier," "lighter"), or describe sets of objects by the number of objects in each set. *Number and Operations:* Children use meanings of numbers to create strategies for solving problems and responding to practical situations, such as getting just enough napkins for a group, or mathematical situations, such as determining that any shape is a triangle if it has exactly three straight sides and is closed. *Algebra:* Children recognize and duplicate simple sequential patterns (e.g., square, circle, square, circle, square, circle,…).

Source: Reprinted from *Curriculum Focal Points for Prekindergarten through Grade 8 Mathematics: A Quest for Coherence* (Reston, Va.: National Council of Teachers of Mathematics, 2006, p. 11).

Appendix B

Curriculum Focal Points and Connections for Kindergarten

The set of three curriculum focal points and related connections for mathematics in kindergarten follow. These topics are the recommended content emphases for this grade level. It is essential that these focal points be addressed in contexts that promote problem solving, reasoning, communication, making connections, and designing and analyzing representations.

Kindergarten Curriculum Focal Points	Connections to the Focal Points
Number and Operations: **Representing, comparing, and ordering whole numbers and joining and separating sets** Children use numbers, including written numerals, to represent quantities and to solve quantitative problems, such as counting objects in a set, creating a set with a given number of objects, comparing and ordering sets or numerals by using both cardinal and ordinal meanings, and modeling simple joining and separating situations with objects. They choose, combine, and apply effective strategies for answering quantitative questions, including quickly recognizing the number in a small set, counting and producing sets of given sizes, counting the number in combined sets, and counting backward.	*Data Analysis:* Children sort objects and use one or more attributes to solve problems. For example, they might sort solids that roll easily from those that do not. Or they might collect data and use counting to answer such questions as, "What is our favorite snack?" They re-sort objects by using new attributes (e.g., after sorting solids according to which ones roll, they might re-sort the solids according to which ones stack easily). *Geometry:* Children integrate their understandings of geometry, measurement, and number. For example, they understand, discuss, and create simple navigational directions (e.g., "Walk forward 10 steps, turn right, and walk forward 5 steps"). *Algebra:* Children identify, duplicate, and extend simple number patterns and sequential and growing patterns (e.g., patterns made with shapes) as preparation for creating rules that describe relationships.
Geometry: **Describing shapes and space** Children interpret the physical world with geometric ideas (e.g., shape, orientation, spatial relations) and describe it with corresponding vocabulary. They identify, name, and describe a variety of shapes, such as squares, triangles, circles, rectangles, (regular) hexagons, and (isosceles) trapezoids presented in a variety of ways (e.g., with different sizes or orientations), as well as such three-dimensional shapes as spheres, cubes, and cylinders. They use basic shapes and spatial reasoning to model objects in their environment and to construct more complex shapes.	
Measurement: **Ordering objects by measurable attributes** Children use measurable attributes, such as length or weight, to solve problems by comparing and ordering objects. They compare the lengths of two objects both directly (by comparing them with each other) and indirectly (by comparing both with a third object), and they order several objects according to length.	

Source: Reprinted from *Curriculum Focal Points for Prekindergarten through Grade 8 Mathematics: A Quest for Coherence* (Reston, Va.: National Council of Teachers of Mathematics, 2006, p. 12).

Appendix C

Curriculum Focal Points and Connections for Grade 1

The set of three curriculum focal points and related connections for mathematics in grade 1 follow. These topics are the recommended content emphases for this grade level. It is essential that these focal points be addressed in contexts that promote problem solving, reasoning, communication, making connections, and designing and analyzing representations.

Grade 1 Curriculum Focal Points	Connections to the Focal Points
Number and Operations and *Algebra:* **Developing understandings of addition and subtraction and strategies for basic addition facts and related subtraction facts** Children develop strategies for adding and subtracting whole numbers on the basis of their earlier work with small numbers. They use a variety of models, including discrete objects, length-based models (e.g., lengths of connecting cubes), and number lines, to model "part-whole," "adding to," "taking away from," and "comparing" situations to develop an understanding of the meanings of addition and subtraction and strategies to solve such arithmetic problems. Children understand the connections between counting and the operations of addition and subtraction (e.g., adding two is the same as "counting on" two). They use properties of addition (commutativity and associativity) to add whole numbers, and they create and use increasingly sophisticated strategies based on these properties (e.g., "making tens") to solve addition and subtraction problems involving basic facts. By comparing a variety of solution strategies, children relate addition and subtraction as inverse operations.	*Number and Operations* and *Algebra:* Children use mathematical reasoning, including ideas such as commutativity and associativity and beginning ideas of tens and ones, to solve two-digit addition and subtraction problems with strategies that they understand and can explain. They solve both routine and nonroutine problems. *Measurement* and *Data Analysis:* Children strengthen their sense of number by solving problems involving measurements and data. Measuring by laying multiple copies of a unit end to end and then counting the units by using groups of tens and ones supports children's understanding of number lines and number relationships. Representing measurements and discrete data in picture and bar graphs involves counting and comparisons that provide another meaningful connection to number relationships. *Algebra:* Through identifying, describing, and applying number patterns and properties in developing strategies for basic facts, children learn about other properties of numbers and operations, such as odd and even (e.g., "Even numbers of objects can be paired, with none left over"), and 0 as the identity element for addition.
Number and Operations: **Developing an understanding of whole number relationships, including grouping in tens and ones** Children compare and order whole numbers (at least to 100) to develop an understanding of and solve problems involving the relative sizes of these numbers. They think of whole numbers between 10 and 100 in terms of groups of tens and ones (especially recognizing the numbers 11 to 19 as 1 group of ten and particular numbers of ones). They understand the sequential order of the counting numbers and their relative magnitudes and represent numbers on a number line.	
Geometry: **Composing and decomposing geometric shapes** Children compose and decompose plane and solid figures (e.g., by putting two congruent isosceles triangles together to make a rhombus), thus building an understanding of part-whole relationships as well as the properties of the original and composite shapes. As they combine figures, they recognize them from different perspectives and orientations, describe their geometric attributes and properties, and determine how they are alike and different, in the process developing a background for measurement and initial understandings of such properties as congruence and symmetry.	

Source: Reprinted from *Curriculum Focal Points for Prekindergarten through Grade 8 Mathematics: A Quest for Coherence* (Reston, Va.: National Council of Teachers of Mathematics, 2006, p. 13).

Appendix D

Curriculum Focal Points and Connections for Grade 2

The set of three curriculum focal points and related connections for mathematics in grade 2 follow. These topics are the recommended content emphases for this grade level. It is essential that these focal points be addressed in contexts that promote problem solving, reasoning, communication, making connections, and designing and analyzing representations.

Grade 2 Curriculum Focal Points	Connections to the Focal Points
Number and Operations: Developing an understanding of the base-ten numeration system and place-value concepts Children develop an understanding of the base-ten numeration system and place-value concepts (at least to 1000). Their understanding of base-ten numeration includes ideas of counting in units and multiples of hundreds, tens, and ones, as well as a grasp of number relationships, which they demonstrate in a variety of ways, including comparing and ordering numbers. They understand multidigit numbers in terms of place value, recognizing that place-value notation is a shorthand for the sums of multiples of powers of 10 (e.g., 853 as 8 hundreds + 5 tens + 3 ones).	*Number and Operations:* Children use place value and properties of operations to create equivalent representations of given numbers (such as 35 represented by 35 ones, 3 tens and 5 ones, or 2 tens and 15 ones) and to write, compare, and order multidigit numbers. They use these ideas to compose and decompose multidigit numbers. Children add and subtract to solve a variety of problems, including applications involving measurement, geometry, and data, as well as nonroutine problems. In preparation for grade 3, they solve problems involving multiplicative situations, developing initial understandings of multiplication as repeated addition. *Geometry and Measurement:* Children estimate, measure, and compute lengths as they solve problems involving data, space, and movement through space. By composing and decomposing two-dimensional shapes (intentionally substituting arrangements of smaller shapes for larger shapes or substituting larger shapes for many smaller shapes), they use geometric knowledge and spatial reasoning to develop foundations for understanding area, fractions, and proportions. *Algebra:* Children use number patterns to extend their knowledge of properties of numbers and operations. For example, when skip counting, they build foundations for understanding multiples and factors.
Number and Operations and Algebra: Developing quick recall of addition facts and related subtraction facts and fluency with multidigit addition and subtraction Children use their understanding of addition to develop quick recall of basic addition facts and related subtraction facts. They solve arithmetic problems by applying their understanding of models of addition and subtraction (such as combining or separating sets or using number lines), relationships and properties of number (such as place value), and properties of addition (commutativity and associativity). Children develop, discuss, and use efficient, accurate, and generalizable methods to add and subtract multidigit whole numbers. They select and apply appropriate methods to estimate sums and differences or calculate them mentally, depending on the context and numbers involved. They develop fluency with efficient procedures, including standard algorithms, for adding and subtracting whole numbers, understand why the procedures work (on the basis of place value and properties of operations), and use them to solve problems.	
Measurement: Developing an understanding of linear measurement and facility in measuring lengths Children develop an understanding of the meaning and processes of measurement, including such underlying concepts as partitioning (the mental activity of slicing the length of an object into equal-sized units) and transitivity (e.g., if object A is longer than object B and object B is longer than object C, then object A is longer than object C). They understand linear measure as an iteration of units and use rulers and other measurement tools with that understanding. They understand the need for equal-length units, the use of standard units of measure (centimeter and inch), and the inverse relationship between the size of a unit and the number of units used in a particular measurement (i.e., children recognize that the smaller the unit, the more iterations they need to cover a given length).	

36

Source: Reprinted from *Curriculum Focal Points for Prekindergarten through Grade 8 Mathematics: A Quest for Coherence* (Reston, Va.: National Council of Teachers of Mathematics, 2006, p. 14).

Appendix E

Sample State Curriculum for Grade 1 Organized around Focal Points

K–8 MATHEMATICS STANDARDS
GRADE 1

BIG IDEA 1: *Develop understandings of addition and subtraction strategies for basic addition facts and related subtraction facts.*

BENCHMARK CODE	BENCHMARK
MA.1.A.1.1	Model addition and subtraction situations using the concepts of "part-whole," "adding to," "taking away from," "comparing," and "missing addend."
MA.1.A.1.2	Identify, describe, and apply addition and subtraction as inverse operations.
MA.1.A.1.3	Create and use increasingly sophisticated strategies, and use properties such as Commutative, Associative and Additive Identity, to add whole numbers.
MA.1.A.1.4	Use counting strategies, number patterns, and models as a means for solving basic addition and subtraction fact problems.

Access Points for Students with Significant Cognitive Disabilities		
Independent:	*Supported:*	*Participatory:*
MA.1.A.1.In.a Identify the meaning of addition as adding to and subtraction as taking away from.	MA.1.A.1.Su.a Demonstrate understanding of the meaning of joining (putting together) and separating (taking apart) sets of objects.	MA.1.A.1.Pa.a Respond to the arrival of a familiar person or addition of a familiar object in a routine.
MA.1.A.1.In.b Use counting and one-to-one correspondence as strategies to solve addition facts with sums to 10 and related subtraction facts represented by numerals with sets of objects and pictures.	MA.1.A.1.Su.b Use one-to-one correspondence as a strategy for solving simple number stories involving joining (putting together) and separating (taking apart) with sets of objects to 5.	MA.1.A.1.Pa.b Respond to the departure of a familiar person or removal of a familiar object in a routine.

From *2007 Florida Sunshine State Standards for Mathematics*. Reprinted with permission from Florida State Department of Education.

Sample State Curriculum for Grade 1
Organized around Focal Points
—Continued

BIG IDEA 2: *Develop an understanding of whole number relationships, including grouping by tens and ones.*	
BENCHMARK CODE	**BENCHMARK**
MA.1.A.2.1	Compare and order whole numbers at least to 100.
MA.1.A.2.2	Represent two-digit numbers in terms of tens and ones.
MA.1.A.2.3	Order counting numbers, compare their relative magnitudes, and represent numbers on a number line.

Access Points for Students with Significant Cognitive Disabilities

Independent:	Supported:	Participatory:
MA.1.A.2.In.a Compare and order numbers 1 to 10. MA.1.A.2.In.b Use one-to-one correspondence to count sets of objects or pictures to 10. MA.1.A.2.In.c Represent numbers to 10 using sets of objects and pictures, number names, and numerals.	MA.1.A.2.Su.a Use one-to-one correspondence to compare sets of objects to 5. MA.1.A.2.Su.b Use one-to-one correspondence to count sets of objects to 5 arranged in a row. MA.1.A.2.Su.c Represent quantities to 5 using sets of objects and number names.	MA.1.A.2.Pa.a Respond to a prompt to indicate desire for more of two or more preferred actions or objects in a familiar routine. MA.1.A.2.Pa.b Respond to a prompt to indicate desire to stop two or more actions in a familiar routine. MA.1.A.2.Pa.c Respond to a counting cue to begin two or more familiar routines.

From *2007 Florida Sunshine State Standards for Mathematics.* Reprinted with permission from Florida State Department of Education.

Sample State Curriculum for Grade 1
Organized around Focal Points
—Continued

BIG IDEA 3: *Compose and decompose two-dimensional and three-dimensional geometric shapes.*	
BENCHMARK CODE	**BENCHMARK**
MA.1.G.3.1	Use appropriate vocabulary to compare shapes according to attributes and properties such as number and lengths of sides, and number of vertices.
MA.1.G.3.2	Compose and decompose plane and solid figures, including making predictions about them, to build an understanding of part-whole relationships and properties of shapes.

Access Points for Students with Significant Cognitive Disabilities

Independent:	Supported:	Participatory:
MA.1.G.3.In.a Sort and describe two-dimensional shapes by single attributes such as number of sides and straight or round sides.	MA.1.G.3.Su.a Match common two-dimensional objects by shape, including square and circle.	MA.1.G.3.Pa.a Respond to a prompt to identify a familiar object with a two-dimensional shape, such as circle or square in familiar routines.
MA.1.G.3.In.b Identify examples of three-dimensional objects, including sphere and cube.	MA.1.G.3.Su.b Name two-dimensional shapes, including circle and square. MA.1.G.3.Su.c Sort common two- and three-dimensional objects by size, including big and little.	MA.1.G.3.Pa.b Respond to a prompt to identify two or more familiar three-dimensional objects in familiar routines.
MA.1.G.3.In.c Combine two shapes to make another shape and identify the whole-part relationship.	MA.1.G.3.Su.d Identify spatial relationships, including in, out, top, and bottom.	MA.1.G.3.Pa.c Demonstrate awareness of one discrete location (area) in the learning environment.
MA.1.G.3.In.d Describe spatial relationships, including *over, under, front, back,* and *between.*		MA.1.G.3.Pa.d Respond to two-directional prompts in familiar routines.

From *2007 Florida Sunshine State Standards for Mathematics.* Reprinted with permission from Florida State Department of Education.

Sample State Curriculum for Grade 1
Organized around Focal Points
—Continued

SUPPORTING IDEAS	
Algebra	

BENCHMARK CODE	BENCHMARK
MA.1.A.4.1	Extend repeating and growing patterns, fill in missing terms, and justify reasoning.

Access Points for Students with Significant Cognitive Disabilities		
Independent:	**Supported:**	**Participatory:**
MA.1.A.4. In.a Match a two-element repeating visual pattern.	MA.1.A.4.Su.a Match objects by single attributes such as color, shape, or size.	MA.1.A.4.Pa.a Indicate anticipation of next step in a familiar routine or activity.

SUPPORTING IDEAS	
Geometry and Measurement	

BENCHMARK CODE	BENCHMARK
MA.1.G.5.1	Measure by using iterations of a unit and count the unit measures by grouping units.
MA.1.G.5.2	Compare and order objects according to descriptors of length, weight and capacity.

Access Points for Students with Significant Cognitive Disabilities		
Independent:	**Supported:**	**Participatory:**
MA.1.G.5.In.a Measure length of objects using nonstandard units of measure and count the units.	MA.1.G.5.Su.a Measure length of objects using nonstandard units of measure.	MA.1.G.5.Pa.a Respond to differences in familiar persons, actions, or objects in two or more familiar routines.
MA.1.G.5.In.b Compare objects by concepts of length, using terms like longer, shorter, and same; and capacity, using terms like full and empty.	MA.1.G.5.Su.b Compare objects by length using terms like long and short.	MA.1.G.5.Pa.b Respond to the environmental cue for preferred activities within regularly scheduled routines.
MA.1.G.5.In.c Identify concepts of time, including before, after, and next, by relating daily events to a time period.	MA.1.G.5.Su.c Identify the concepts of time, including morning and afternoon, by relating daily events to a time period.	

From *2007 Florida Sunshine State Standards for Mathematics*. Reprinted with permission from Florida State Department of Education.

Sample State Curriculum for Grade 1
Organized around Focal Points
—*Continued*

SUPPORTING IDEAS	
Number and Operations	

BENCHMARK CODE	BENCHMARK
MA.1.A.6.1	Use mathematical reasoning and beginning understanding of tens and ones, including the use of invented strategies, to solve two-digit addition and subtraction problems
MA.1.A.6.2	Solve routine and non-routine problems by acting them out, using manipulatives, and drawing diagrams

Access Points for Students with Significant Cognitive Disabilities		
Independent:	*Supported:*	*Participatory:*
MA.1.A.6.In.a Solve real-world problems involving addition facts with sums to 10 and related subtraction facts using numerals with sets of objects and pictures.	MA.1.A.6.Su.a Solve real-world problems involving simple joining (putting together) and separating (taking apart) situations with sets of objects to 5.	MA.1.A.6.Pa.a Demonstrate distinctive responses to preferred vs. non-preferred stimuli in two familiar routines.

From *2007 Florida Sunshine State Standards for Mathematics.* Reprinted with permission from Florida State Department of Education.

Appendix F

A Roadmap to the NCTM Navigations Series from the Prekindergarten, Kindergarten, Grade 1, and Grade 2 Curriculum Focal Points

Developing and implementing a program of instruction for prekindergarten through grade 2 calls for a wide variety of resources. One resource that offers curriculum planners and teachers special assistance is the **Navigations Series,** published by the National Council of Teachers of Mathematics. Each book in this popular series provides classroom teachers with ideas and suggestions for presenting essential, Standards-based content through lively hands-on activities for students. A CD-ROM, filled with rich supplemental materials for teachers and students alike, accompanies each volume. The books expand and illustrate the vision of mathematics instruction outlined in **Principles and Standards for School Mathematics,** a landmark publication that identified six Principles that form the foundation of any high-quality program of mathematics instruction: Equity, Curriculum, Teaching, Learning, Assessment, and Technology.

NCTM's recently released **Curriculum Focal Points for Prekindergarten through Grade 8 Mathematics: A Quest for Coherence** demonstrates how schools can apply the Curriculum Principle in prekindergarten–grade 8. Already recognized as an influential force in curriculum development across the country, **Curriculum Focal Points** identifies important mathematical topics for each grade level, Pre-K–8, and encapsulates these in a set of Focal Points that can serve to organize curriculum design and instruction at and across grade levels.

Numerous materials from the Navigations Series can help in building a coherent, comprehensive curriculum that will prepare prekindergarten students in very direct ways for future mathematics—particularly algebra. The books and activities identified below support each Focal Point indentified in **Curriculum Focal Points** for prekindergarten–grade 2. The materials listed are just a sampling of the resources that the Navigations Series offers in support of core instruction at these grade levels. Recommended materials appear beneath the Focal Points and their descriptions from **Curriculum Focal Points.** Each Focal Point is marked by a bullet. **Curriculum Focal Points** also identifies Connections to the Focal Points at each grade level. Materials in the Navigations Series that support the Connections for prekindergarten–grade 2 appear at the end of the respective "roadmaps" for those grades.

Curriculum Focal Points	Prekindergarten

- **Number and Operations: Developing an understanding of whole numbers, including concepts of correspondence, counting, cardinality, and comparison**

Children develop an understanding of the meanings of whole numbers and recognize the number of objects in small groups without counting and by counting—the first and most basic mathematical algorithm. They understand that number words refer to quantity. They use one-to-one correspondence to solve problems by matching sets and comparing the number amounts and in counting objects to 10 and beyond. They understand that the last word that they state in counting tells "how many," they count to determine number amounts and compare quantities (using language such as "more than" and "less than"), and they order sets by the number of objects in them.

Navigating through Number and Operations in Prekindergarten–Grade 2 (Cavanagh, Mary, Linda Dacey, Carol R. Findell, Carole E. Greenes, Linda Jensen Sheffield, and Marian Small, edited by Carole E. Greenes, 2004; NCTM stock number 12538)

Overview	Introduction (pages 1–11), chapter 1 (pages 13–15), chapter 2 (pages 37–40), chapter 3 (pages 59–61)
Ordering	"Ducks in a Line" (pages 21–22)
Counting	"Frumps' Fashions" (pages 41–45)
Counting	"Frames" (pages 46–48)

Navigating through Algebra in Prekindergarten–Grade 2 (Greenes, Carole E., Mary Cavanagh, Linda Dacey, Carol R. Findell, and Marian Small, edited by Carole E. Greenes, 2001; NCTM stock number 752)

Overview	Introduction (pages 1–5), chapter 1 (pages 7–9), chapter 2 (pages 31–33), chapter 3 (pages 53–54)
Counting	"Clown Line-Up" (pages 10–12)
Sequencing	"Snakes and More Snakes" (pages 13–15)
Counting to Ten	"How Many Are under the Cup?" (pages 34–35)
Comparing	"Tall Towers" (pages 55–56)

- **Geometry: Identifying shapes and describing spatial relationships**

Children develop spatial reasoning by working from two perspectives on space as they examine the shapes of objects and inspect their relative positions. They find shapes in their environments and describe them in their own words. They build pictures and designs by combining two- and three-dimensional shapes, and they solve such problems as deciding which piece will fit into a space in a puzzle. They discuss the relative positions of objects with vocabulary such as "above," "below," and "next to."

Navigating through Geometry in Prekindergarten–Grade 2 (Findell, Carol R., Marian Small, Mary Cavanagh, Linda Dacey, Carole E. Greenes, and Linda Jensen Sheffield, edited by Carol E. Greenes, 2001; NCTM stock number 12140)

Overview	Introduction (pages 1–8), chapter 1 (pages 9–13), chapter 2 (pages 31–32), chapter 3 (pages 49–51), chapter 4 (pages 67–68)
Shapes	"Shapes from Shapes" (pages 14–16)
Shapes	"Alike and Different" (pages 17–18)
Position	"Ins and Outs" (pages 33–35)
Reflections	"Mirror Monsters" (pages 52–54)

- **Measurement: Identifying measurable attributes and comparing objects by using these attributes**

Children identify objects as "the same" or "different," and then "more" or less," on the basis of attributes they can measure. They identify measurable attributes such as length and weight and solve problems by making direct comparisons of objects on the basis of those attributes.

Navigating through Measurement in Prekindergarten–Grade 2 (Dacey, Linda, Mary Cavanagh, Carol R. Findell, Carole E. Greenes, Linda Jensen Sheffield, and Marian Small, edited by Carole E. Greenes, 2003; NCTM stock number 12523)

Overview	Introduction (pages 1–10), chapter 1 (pages 11–13), chapter 2 (pages 29–31)
Comparing	"Body Balance" (pages 14–15)
Comparing	"Scavenger Hunt" (pages 16–17)
Length	"Giant Steps, Baby Steps" (pages 32–33)

Connections to the Focal Points: Prekindergarten

Navigating through Data Analysis and Probability in Prekindergarten–Grade 2 (Sheffield, Linda Jensen, Mary Cavanagh, Linda Dacey, Carol R. Findell, Carole E. Greenes, and Marian Small, edited by Carole E. Greenes, 2002; NCTM stock number 12323)

Overview	Introduction (pages 1–10), chapter 1 (pages 11–14), chapter 2 (pages 41–43), chapter 3 (pages 63–64)
Graphs	"Build a Graph" (pages 15–17)
Tables and Graphs	"What's Your Favorite" (pages 18–21)
Sort and Compare	"Junk Sort" (pages 22–24)
Likelihood	"Possible or Impossible" (pages 65–66)

Navigating through Problem Solving and Reasoning in Prekindergarten–Kindergarten (Greenes, Carole E., Linda Dacey, Mary Cavanagh, Carol R. Findell, Linda Jensen Sheffield, and Marian Small, edited by Carole E. Greenes, 2003; NCTM stock number 12582)

Overview	Introduction (pages 1–7)
Counting	"Bears in the House and in the Park" (pages 10–13)
Geometric Relationships	"Shape Families" (pages 17–19)
Measurement	"Line Up" (pages 20–22)

Curriculum Focal Points | Kindergarten

- **Number and Operations: Representing, comparing, and ordering whole numbers and joining and separating sets**

  Children use numbers, including written numerals, to represent quantities and to solve quantitative problems, such as counting objects in a set, creating a set with a given number of objects, comparing and ordering sets or numerals by using both cardinal and ordinal meanings, and modeling simple joining and separating situations with objects. They choose, combine, and apply effective strategies for answering quantitative questions, including quickly recognizing the numbers in a small set, counting and producing sets of given sizes, counting the number in combined sets, and counting backward.

Navigating through Number and Operations in Prekindergarten–Grade 2 (Cavanagh, Mary, Linda Dacey, Carol R. Findell, Carole E. Greenes, Linda Jensen Sheffield, and Marian Small, edited by Carole E. Greenes, 2004; NCTM stock number 12538)

Overview	Introduction (pages 1–12), chapter 1 (pages 13–15), chapter 2 (pages 37–40), chapter 3 (pages 59–61)
Representation	"Choose a Number" (pages 16–18)
Combining	"Frumps' Fashions" (pages 41–45)
Joining Sets	"Frames" (pages 46–48)
Equal-sized Groups	"Jamal's Balloons" (pages 52–54)
Addition	"Flip Two" (pages 65–67)

- **Geometry: Describing shapes and space**

  Children interpret the physical world with geometric ideas (e.g., shape, orientation, spatial relationships) and describe it with corresponding vocabulary. They identify, name, and describe a variety of shapes, such as squares, triangles, circles, rectangles, (regular) hexagons, and (isosceles) trapezoids presented in a variety of ways (e.g., with different sizes or orientations), as well as such three-dimensional shapes as spheres, cubes, and cylinders. They use basic shapes and spatial reasoning to model objects in their environment and to construct more complex shapes.

Navigating through Geometry in Prekindergarten–Grade 2 (Findell, Carol R., Marian Small, Mary Cavanagh, Linda Dacey, Carole E. Greenes, and Linda Jensen Sheffield, edited by Carol E. Greenes, 2001; NCTM stock number 12140)

Overview	Introduction (pages 1–8), chapter 1 (pages 9–13), chapter 2 (pages 31–33), chapter 3 (pages 49–51), chapter 4 (pages 67–68)
Sorting Shapes	"Alike and Different" (pages 17–18)
Position	"Ins and Outs" (pages 33–35)
Relative Position	"Match My Grid" (pages 36–37)
Spatial Reasoning	"From Here to There" (pages 39–41)
Spatial Reasoning	"Mirror Monsters" (pages 52–54)
Create Shapes	"Mirror Pictures" (pages 55–58)
Basic Shapes	"Block Views" (pages 69–70)

- **Measurement: Ordering objects by measurable attributes**

  Children use measurable attributes, such as length or weight, to solve problems by comparing and ordering objects. They compare the lengths of two objects both directly (by comparing them with each other) and indirectly (by comparing both with a third object), and they order several objects according to length.

Navigating through Measurement in Prekindergarten–Grade 2 (Dacey, Linda, Mary Cavanagh, Carol R. Findell, Carole E. Greenes, Linda Jensen Sheffield, and Marian Small, edited by Carole E. Greenes, 2003; NCTM stock number 12523)

Overview	Introduction (pages 1–10), chapter 1 (pages 11–13), chapter 2 (pages 29–32)
Comparing	"Body Balance" (pages 14–15)
Sizing	"Scavenger Hunt" (pages 16–17)
Capacity	"Fill It Up" (pages 21–23)
Length	"Giant Steps, Baby Steps" (pages 32–33)
Comparing Weights	"Balance the Pans" (pages 34–36)

Unit Measure	"Snake Imprints" (pages 37–40)
Comparing Amounts	"Scoop It" (pages 41–43)
Standard Unit	"Grandma" (pages 49–51)

Connections to the Focal Points: Kindergarten

Navigating through Algebra in Prekindergarten–Grade 2 (Greenes, Carole E., Mary Cavanagh, Linda Dacey, Carol R. Findell, and Marian Small, edited by Carole E. Greenes, 2001; NCTM stock number 752)

Patterns	"Snakes and More Snakes" (pages 13–15)
Patterns	"Footprints" (pages 16–18)
Missing Addends	"How Many Are under the Cup?" (pages 34–35)
Addition Facts	"Lots of Spots" (pages 36–37)
Measurement	"Who Jumps the Farthest?" (pages 57–59)

Navigating through Problem Solving and Reasoning in Prekindergarten–Kindergarten (Greenes, Carole E., Linda Dacey, Mary Cavanagh, Carol R. Findell, Linda Jensen Sheffield, and Marian Small, edited by Carole E. Greenes, 2003; NCTM stock number 12582)

Overview	Introduction (pages 1–7)
Counting	"Bears in the House and in the Park" (pages 10–13)
Geometric Relationships	"Shape Families" (pages 17–19)
Measurement	"Line Up" (pages 20–22)

Curriculum Focal Points · Grade 1

- **Number and Operations and Algebra: Developing understandings of addition and subtraction and strategies for basic addition and related subtraction facts**

    Children develop strategies for adding and subtracting whole numbers on the basis of their earlier work with small numbers. They use a variety of models, including discrete objects, length-based models (e.g., lengths of connecting cubes), and number lines, to model "part-whole," "adding to," "taking away from," and "comparing" situations to develop an understanding of the meanings of addition and subtraction and strategies to solve such arithmetic problems. Children understand the connections between counting and the operations of addition and subtraction (e.g., adding two is the same as "counting on" two). They use properties of addition (commutativity and associativity) to add whole numbers, and they create and use increasingly sophisticated strategies based on these properties (e.g., "making tens") to solve addition and subtraction problems involving basic facts. By comparing a variety of solution strategies, children relate addition and subtraction as inverse operations.

Navigating through Number and Operations in Prekindergarten–Grade 2 (Cavanagh, Mary, Linda Dacey, Carol R. Findell, Carole E. Greenes, Linda Jensen Sheffield, and Marian Small, edited by Carole E. Greenes, 2004; NCTM stock number 12358)

Overview	Introduction (pages 1–13), chapter 1 (pages 13–15), chapter 2 (pages 37–40), chapter 3 (pages 59–61)
Basic Addition	"Choose a Number" (pages 16–18)
Skip Counting	"Counting in Different Ways" (pages 19–20)
Ordinal Numbers	"Ducks in a Line" (pages 21–22)
Meaning of Operations	"Park Your Car" (pages 49–51)
Equal Groups	"Jamal's Balloons" (pages 52–54)
Properties	"Double Plus or Minus" (pages 62–64)
Basic Facts	"Flip Two" (pages 65–67)
Add and Subtract	"Zooey Lunch" (pages 68–69)
Computation	"Valuable Art" (pages 70–71)
Mental Arithmetic	"One-Out" (pages 82–84)

- **Number and Operations: Developing an understanding of whole-number relationships, including grouping in tens and ones**

  Children compare and order whole numbers (at least to 100) to develop an understanding of and solve problems involving the relative sizes of these numbers. They think of whole numbers between 10 and 100 in terms of tens and ones (especially recognizing the numbers 11 to 19 as one group of ten and a particular number of ones). They understand the sequential order of the counting numbers and their relative magnitudes and represent numbers on a number line.

Navigating through Number and Operations in Prekindergarten–Grade 2 (Cavanagh, Mary, Linda Dacey, Carol R. Findell, Carole E. Greenes, Linda Jensen Sheffield, and Marian Small, edited by Carole E. Greenes, 2004; NCTM stock number 12538)

Overview	Introduction (pages 1–13), chapter 1 (pages 13–15), chapter 2 (pages 37–40), chapter 3 (pages 59–61)
Grouping by Tens	"Trading Up and Down" (pages 23–25)
Grouping by Tens	"How Many Ways?" (pages 26–28)
Base-ten Computation	"Make a Match" (pages 76–78)

- **Geometry: Composing and decomposing geometric shapes**

Navigating through Geometry in Prekindergarten–Grade 2 (Findell, Carol R., Marian Small, Mary Cavanagh, Linda Dacey, Carole E. Greenes, and Linda Jensen Sheffield, edited by Carol E. Greenes, 2001; NCTM stock number 12140)

Overview	Introduction (pages 1–8), chapter 1 (pages 9–13), chapter 2 (pages 31–33), chapter 3 (pages 49–51), chapter 4 (pages 67–68)
Naming Shapes	"Cutting Corners" (pages 22–25)
Recognizing Shapes	"Match My Grid" (pages 36–38)
Translations	"From Here to There" (pages 39–41)
Mapping	"Map Maker" (pages 42–44)
Reflections	"Mirror Pictures" (pages 55–58)
Symmetry	"Building Shapes" (pages 59–61)
Symmetry	"Cutouts" (pages 73–75)
Spatial Relationships	"Design Tiles" (pages 62–63)
Recognizing Shapes and Objects	"Projector Math" (pages 71–72)

Connections to the Focal Points: Grade 1

Navigating through Algebra in Prekindergarten–Grade 2 (Greenes, Carole E., Mary Cavanagh, Linda Dacey, Carol R. Findell, and Marian Small, edited by Carole E. Greenes, 2001; NCTM Stock Number 752)

Patterns	"Footprints" (pages 16–18)
Number Patterns	"Follow the Number Roads" (pages 19–21)
Number Patterns	"Rows and Rows" (pages 65–67)
Extending Patterns	"How Does It Grow?" (pages 24–25)
Number Sentences	"Lots of Spots" (pages 36–37)
Properties	"Colorful Combinations" (pages 38–40)
Basic Facts	"Spin Once, Spin Twice" (pages 62–64)

Navigating through Problem Solving and Reasoning in Grade 1 (Findell, Carol R., Mary Cavanagh, Linda Dacey, Carole E. Greenes, Linda Jensen Sheffield, and Marian Small, edited by Carolle E. Greenes, 2004; NCTM stock number 12583)

Overview	Introduction (pages 1–7)
Counting in Groups	"Creature Features" (pages 13–15)
Geometric Reasoning	"Inside or Outside?" (pages 16–19)
Applying Addition	"Which Town Is Which?" (pages 20–22)

Curriculum Focal Points | Grade 2

- **Number and Operations: Developing an understanding of the base-ten numeration system and place-value operations**

Children develop an understanding of the base-ten numeration system and place-value concepts (at least to 1000). Their understanding of base-ten numeration includes ideas of counting in units and multiples of hundreds, tens, and ones, as well as a grasp of number relationships, which they demonstrate in a variety of ways, including comparing and ordering numbers. They understand multidigit numbers in terms of place value, recognizing that place-value notation is a shorthand for the sums of multiples of the powers of ten (e.g., 853 as 8 hundreds + 5 tens + 3 ones).

Navigating through Number and Operations in Prekindergarten–Grade 2 (Cavanagh, Mary, Linda Dacey, Carol R. Findell, Carole E. Greenes, Linda Jensen Sheffield, and Marian Small, edited by Carole E. Greenes, 2004; NCTM stock number 12538)

Overview	Introduction (pages 1–11), chapter 1 (pages 13–15), chapter 2 (pages 37–40), chapter 3 (pages 59–61)
Adding 10 or 100	"Trading Up or Down" (pages 23–25)
Place Value	"How Many Ways?" (pages 26–27)
Place Value	"Make a Match" (pages 76–78)
Order	"All in Order" (pages 29–32)

- **Number and Operations and Algebra: Developing quick recall of addition facts and related subtraction facts and fluency with multidigit addition and subtraction**

Children use their understanding of addition to develop quick recall of basic addition facts and related subtraction facts. They solve arithmetic problems by applying their understanding of models of addition and subtraction (such as combining and separating sets or using the number line), relationships and properties of number (such as place value), and properties of addition (commutativity and associativity). Children develop, discuss, and use efficient, accurate, and generalizable methods to add and subtract multidigit whole numbers. They select and apply appropriate methods to estimate sums and differences or calculate them mentally, depending on the context and numbers involved. They develop fluency with efficient procedures, including standard algorithms, for adding and subtracting whole numbers, understand why the procedures work (on the basis of place value and properties of operations), and use them to solve problems.

Navigating through Number and Operations in Prekindergarten–Grade 2 (Cavanagh, Mary, Linda Dacey, Carol R. Findell, Carole E. Greenes, Linda Jensen Sheffield, and Marian Small, edited by Carole E. Greenes, 2004; NCTM stock number 12538)

Overview	Introduction (pages 1–11), chapter 1 (pages 13–15), chapter 2 (pages 37–40), chapter 3 (pages 59–61)
Basic Multiples	"Counting in Different Ways" (pages 19–20)
Operations	"Park Your Car" (pages 49–51)
Adding Multiples	"Mirror Multiplication" (pages 55–57)
Doubles	"Double Plus or Minus" (pages 62–64)
Computation	"Valuable Art" (pages 70–72)
Computation	"Hit the Target" (pages 79–81)
Mental Math	"Four in a Row" (pages 73–75)
Basic Facts	"One-Out" (pages 82–84)

- **Measurement: Developing an understanding of linear measurement and facility in measuring lengths**

Children develop an understanding of the meaning and process of measurement, including such underlying concepts as partitioning (the mental activity of slicing the length of an object into equal-sized units) and transitivity (e.g., if object A is longer than object B and object B is longer than object C, then object A is longer than object C). They understand linear measure as an iteration of units and use rulers and other measurement tools with that understanding. They understand the need for equal-length units, the use of standard units of measure (centimeter and inch), and the inverse relationship between the size of a unit and the number of units used in a particular measurement (i.e., children recognize that the smaller the unit, the more iterations they need to cover a given length).

Navigating through Measurement in Prekindergarten–Grade 2 (Dacey, Linda, Mary Cavanagh, Carol R. Findell, Carole E. Greenes, Linda Jensen Sheffield, and Marian Small, edited by Carole E. Greenes, 2003; NCTM stock number 12523)

Overview	Introduction (pages 1–9), chapter 1 (pages 11–13), chapter 2 (pages 29–31)
Comparing Length	"Ribbon Heights" (pages 24–26)
Distance	"Snail Trails" (pages 44–46)
Measuring	"Estimation Challenge" (pages 47–48)
Measuring	"How Many in a _____?" (pages 54–58)
Standard Units	"Which Unit Did I Use?" (pages 59–61)
Appropriate Units	"Fit the Facts" (pages 62–63)

Connections to the Focal Points: Grade 2

Navigating through Algebra in Prekindergarten–Grade 2 (Greenes, Carole E., Mary Cavanagh, Linda Dacey, Carol R. Findell, and Marian Small, edited by Carole E. Greenes, 2001; NCTM stock number 90752)

Patterns	"Jumping Rules" (pages 22–23)
Patterns	"How Does It Grow?" (pages 24–26)
Patterns	"Rows and Rows" (pages 65–68)
Equations	"Block Pounds" (pages 44–46)
Equality	"Balancing Act" (pages 47–49)

Navigating through Geometry in Prekindergarten–Grade 2 (Findell, Carol R., Marian Small, Mary Cavanagh, Linda Dacey, Carole E. Greenes, and Linda Jensen Sheffield, edited by Carol E. Greenes, 2001; NCTM stock number 12140)

Shapes	"Cutting Corners" (pages 22–25)
3-D/2-D	"Rolling Nets" (pages 27–30)
Mapping	"Map Making" (pages 42–44)
Symmetry	"Folding Shapes" (pages 59–61)
Symmetry	"Cutouts" (pages 73–75)

Navigating through Problem Solving and Reasoning in Grade 2 (Small, Marian, Linda Jensen Sheffield, Mary Cavanagh, Linda Dacey, Carol R. Findell, and Carole E. Greenes, edited by Carole E. Greenes, 2004; NCTM stock number 12584)

Overview	Introduction (pages 1–5)
Number Relationships	"Piggy Bank" (pages 10–12)
Mental Math	"What's the Sum?" (pages 13–14)
Shapes	"Match Me" (pages 15–18)
Measurement	"From Small to Tall" (pages 19–22)

Appendix G: Sample Student Work
Bracelets Problem

Task

Lisa is making bracelets. She has already made 8 bracelets.

She needs to make 12 all together so she can give one to each of her cousins.

How many more bracelets does she need to make?

Show how you solved this problem. Use pictures, numbers, and words.

Sample Work 1

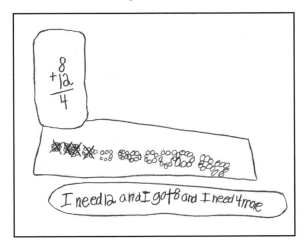

I need 12 and I got 8 and I need 4 more

Sample Work 2

4 to get to 12.

8+4=12

Sample Work 3

She is bone with 8 bracelets. She needs to make 12 more how many Does that make 21

Source: *Mathematics Assessment Sampler, Prekindergarten–Grade 2* (Huinker 2006, pp. 24–27).

Packages of Gum Problem

Task
Robin has 3 packages of gum. Each package has 5 pieces of gum.
How many pieces of gum does Robin have altogether?
Draw a picture to show how much gum Robin has. Find the answer, and write a number sentence to solve the problem.

Sample Work 1

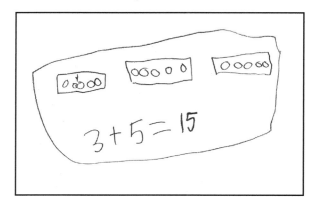

Sample Work 2

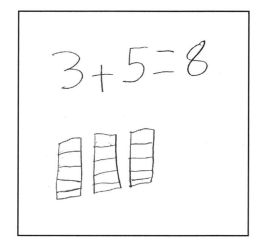

Sample Work 3

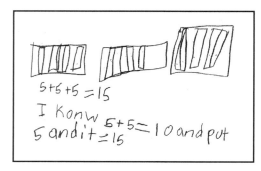

Source: *Mathematics Assessment Sampler, Prekindergarten–Grade 2* (Huinker 2006, pp. 42–45).

All about Triangles Task

Task
Mark all the triangles on the page.
Tell how you know that they are triangles.

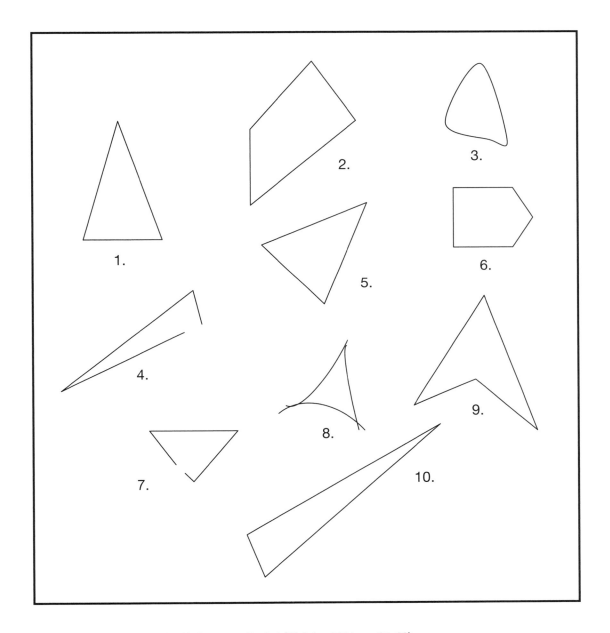

Source: *Mathematics Assessment Sampler, Prekindergarten–Grade 2* (Huinker 2006, pp. 96–99).

All about Triangles Task—*Continued*

Sample Work 1

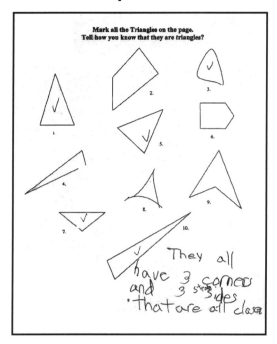

Sample Work 2

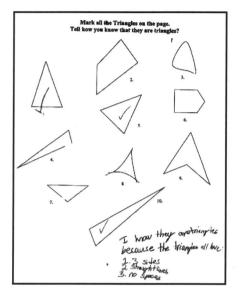

Sample Work 3

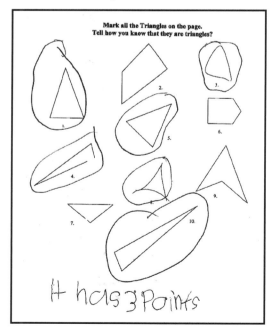

Footsteps Problem

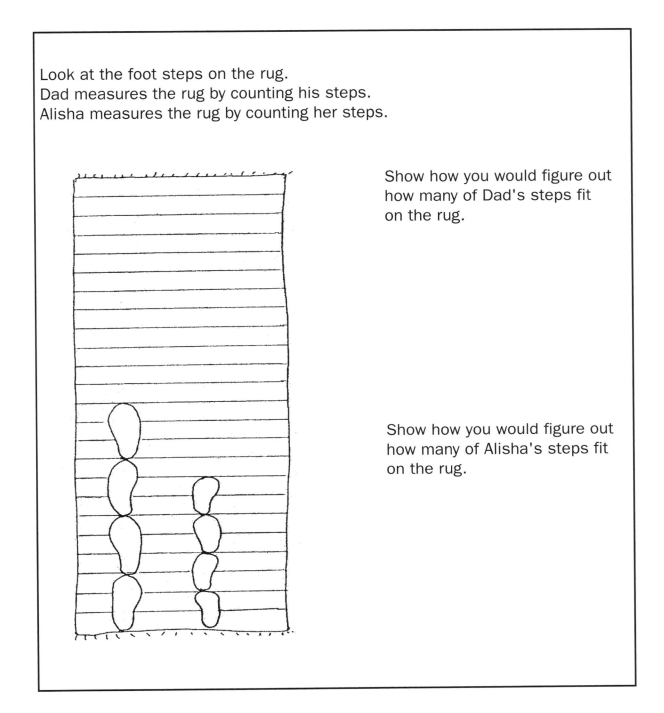

Look at the foot steps on the rug.
Dad measures the rug by counting his steps.
Alisha measures the rug by counting her steps.

Show how you would figure out how many of Dad's steps fit on the rug.

Show how you would figure out how many of Alisha's steps fit on the rug.

Source: *Mathematics Assessment: A Practical Handbook for Grades K–2* (Glanfield, Bush, and Stenmark 2003, p. 146).

Footsteps Problem—*Continued*

Sample Work 1

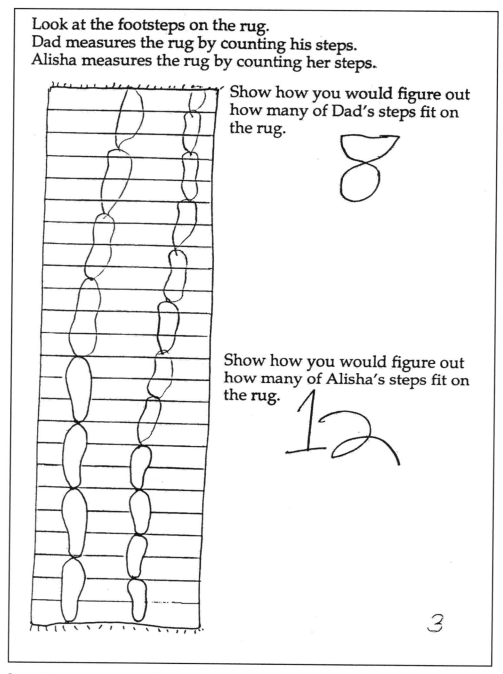

Look at the footsteps on the rug.
Dad measures the rug by counting his steps.
Alisha measures the rug by counting her steps.

Show how you would figure out how many of Dad's steps fit on the rug.

Show how you would figure out how many of Alisha's steps fit on the rug.

Source: *Mathematics Assessment: A Practical Handbook for Grades K–2* (Glanfield, Bush, and Stenmark 2003, p. 130).

Footsteps Problem—*Continued*

Sample Work 2

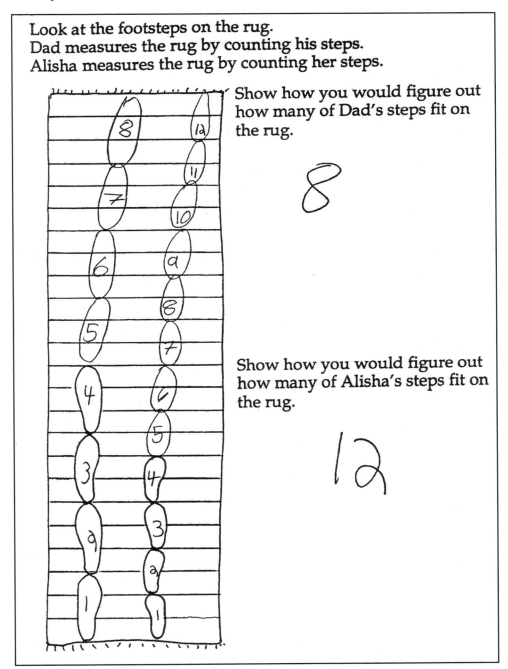

Look at the footsteps on the rug.
Dad measures the rug by counting his steps.
Alisha measures the rug by counting her steps.

Show how you would figure out how many of Dad's steps fit on the rug.

8

Show how you would figure out how many of Alisha's steps fit on the rug.

12

Source: *Mathematics Assessment: A Practical Handbook for Grades K–2* (Glanfield, Bush, and Stenmark 2003, p. 131).

Footsteps Problem—*Continued*

Sample Work 3

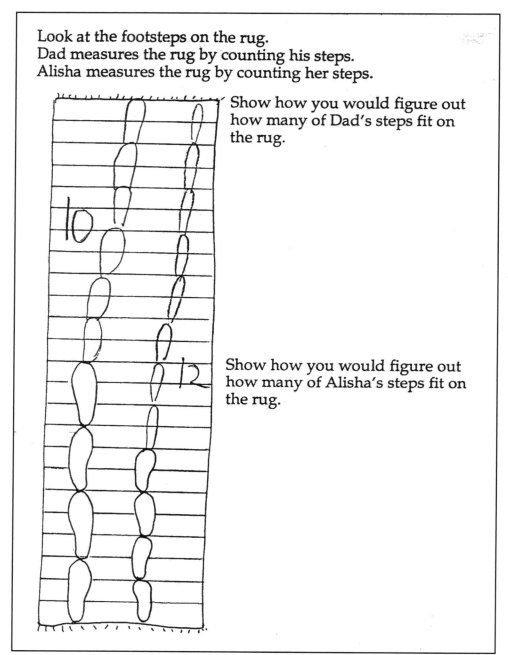

Look at the footsteps on the rug.
Dad measures the rug by counting his steps.
Alisha measures the rug by counting her steps.

Show how you would figure out how many of Dad's steps fit on the rug.

Show how you would figure out how many of Alisha's steps fit on the rug.

Source: *Mathematics Assessment: A Practical Handbook for Grades K–2* (Glanfield, Bush, and Stenmark 2003, p. 128).

Appendix H
Task Sheets

Building-Focus Task

Think about your own grade level or one particular grade level. What are some of the fundamental mathematical ideas or topics that build a foundation for later learning? How do those mathematical ideas or topics connect with learning in later grades?

Development-of-Geometric-Thinking Task

How does geometric thinking develop as students progress from prekindergarten through grade 2? What are other core topics in prekindergarten–grade 2, and how do those topics develop over time? NCTM's *Curriculum Focal Points for Prekindergarten through Grade 8 Mathematics* (2006) and the supporting grade-level books, NCTM's Navigations Series books, and your own curriculum documents are good references to use in this exercise.

Evaluating-My-Curriculum Task

Using your own curriculum for prekindergarten, kindergarten, grade 1, and grade 2 and NCTM's Focal Points (see Appendixes A, B, C, and D), address the following questions:

1. Do I think we currently have a focused mathematics curriculum in prekindergarten–grade 2? Why or Why not?

2. What key ideas or learning progressions can be seen in our existing mathematics curriculum at each grade level? Do any essential ideas appear in NCTM's set of Focal Points that do not appear somewhere in our curriculum, and vice versa? If so, how do we address that discrepancy?

3. Does our sequence of key ideas make sense mathematically? Does it connect logically with the mathematics in earlier and later grade levels and build from grade to grade without unnecessary repetition? If not, how can we change this sequencing?

4. Can we tell from our own curriculum what topics will receive the most emphasis and how these topics are treated differently in prekindergarten, kindergarten, grade 1, and grade 2? How much time would you propose be spent on these areas of emphasis, and should that time be dispersed throughout the year or concentrated?

5. What content areas or topics in our existing curriculum can we think of as "connections" with the identified key ideas? Can we better connect these areas with our key ideas or areas of emphasis instead of teaching them as separate topics?

6. In general, what changes can be made to our curriculum, both overall and within the prekindergarten–grade 2 grade band, to make it more focused?

7. Do our current materials and textbooks support teaching to the depth of understanding required for students' knowledge to grow and deepen over time? What supplemental materials might be used to support this goal?

8. What concerns do I have about the idea of a focused mathematics curriculum in prekindergarten–grade 2?

Questioning Task

Below are a few different classroom assignments that might be given to students in prekindergarten–grade 2. Identify any essential ideas that these activities address. Generate a list of questions that you might ask to focus students' attention on these important ideas and to forge mathematical connections.

Student Assignment 1

Lisa is making bracelets. She has already made 8 bracelets. She needs to make 12 so she can give one to each of her cousins. How many more bracelets does she need to make? Show how you solved this problem. Use pictures, numbers, and words.

Source: *Mathematics Assessment Sampler, Prekindergarten–Grade 2* (Huinker 2006, p. 24).

Essential Ideas   *Teacher Questions*

Student Assignment 2

Robin found some bugs. She gave 5 to her brother and kept 8 to show at school. How many bugs did Robin find? Show how you solved this problem. Use pictures, numbers, and words.

Essential Ideas   *Teacher Questions*

Student Assignment 3

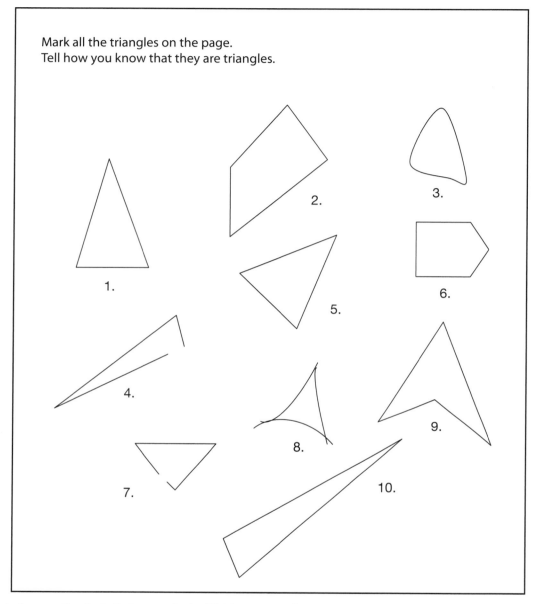

Mark all the triangles on the page.
Tell how you know that they are triangles.

1.
2.
3.
4.
5.
6.
7.
8.
9.
10.

Source: *Mathematics Assessment Sampler, Prekindergarten–Grade 2* (Huinker 2006, p. 96).

Essential Ideas   **Teacher Questions**

Student Assignment 4

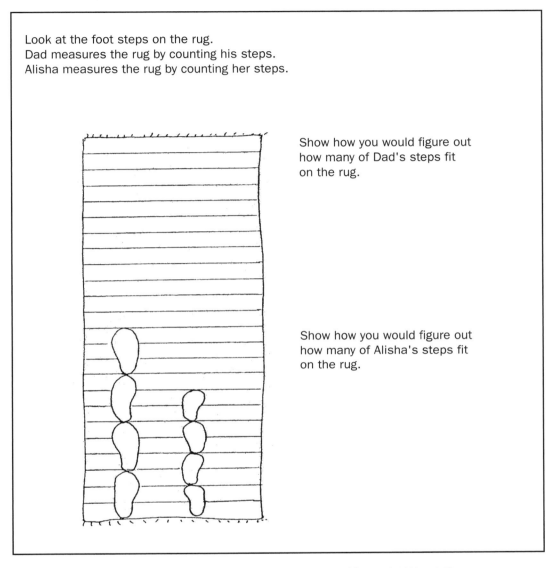

Look at the foot steps on the rug.
Dad measures the rug by counting his steps.
Alisha measures the rug by counting her steps.

Show how you would figure out how many of Dad's steps fit on the rug.

Show how you would figure out how many of Alisha's steps fit on the rug.

Source: *Mathematics Assessment: A Practical Handbook for Grades K–2* (Glanfield, Bush, and Stenmark 2003, p. 146).

Essential Ideas

Teacher Questions

Correcting-Student-Error Task

You notice that many of your students are forgetting to regroup when using the traditional subtraction algorithm. See example below. What questioning or other techniques would you use to help the student correct his or her thinking?

$$
\begin{array}{r}
174 \\
-\ 89 \\
\hline
115
\end{array}
$$

Developing-Depth-of-Understanding Task

Choose a focal point for prekindergarten, kindergarten, grade 1, or grade 2. What kinds of activities might you do with your class to help students acquire depth of understanding?

Subtraction-with-Regrouping Task

Look at these questions:

$$
\begin{array}{r}
52 \\
-\ 25 \\
\hline
\end{array}
\qquad\qquad
\begin{array}{r}
91 \\
-\ 79 \\
\hline
\end{array}
$$

How would you approach these problems if you were teaching second grade? What would you say that pupils would need to understand or be able to do before they could start learning subtraction with regrouping?

Professional-Development-Plan Task

Work with other teachers in your grade or across grades to develop a professional development plan that will support teaching a focused curriculum. Identify short- and long-term goals.

Sample-Student-Work Task

Evaluate the sample student work in Appendix G for depth of understanding. What follow-up questions might you ask the students to get a more complete picture of their reasoning and understanding?

Measuring-Depth-of-Understanding Task

What might constitute an assessment that tries to measure the depth and complexity of one of the Focal Points for prekindergarten, kindergarten, grade 1, or grade 2? Develop a sample assessment task that you might give to students related to that Focal Point.

Appendix I

Sample Answers to Tasks

Building-Focus Task

Answers will vary according to the topics you chose. See the appendix for a listing and descriptions of the Focal Points identified by NCTM for prekindergarten, kindergarten, grade 1, and grade 2.

Development-of-Geometric-Thinking Task

See the summary of the major learning progressions that occur in prekindergarten–grade 2 beginning on page 9.

Evaluating-My-Curriculum Task

Answers will vary because of the wide variation in curricula.

Questioning Task

Student Assignment 1

Essential ideas: This problem supports the grade 1 Focal Point of "Developing understandings of addition and subtraction and strategies for basic addition facts and related subtraction facts." Students' early experiences with addition and subtraction story problems need to involve change problems in which the change is unknown, as in this problem, as well as "joining" and "separating" (i.e., take-away) situations in which an addend is unknown. For students to understand the basic meanings of addition and subtraction, they need to solve the whole range of addition and subtraction problems discussed in the answer to "What are some of the major learning progressions that occur in prekindergarten–grade 2?" beginning on page 9. Most students will represent this situation in some way as an unknown-addend problem $(8 + ? = 12)$ in which the first addend of 8 is known and the total is known, but the second addend (the change amount to be added to the 8) is not known. Another student might use subtraction to solve the problem, understanding that subtracting the eight bracelets she already made from the total number that she needs gives the number of bracelets she still needs to make $(12 - 8 = ?)$. Problems such as this can help students further develop understanding of addition and subtraction and see the relationship between the two operations. Having students act out various addition and subtraction story problems or draw pictures of the scenario given helps students better understand the context of the problem and how the problem might be solved. Even first-grade students should be prompted to make simple mathematical drawings of a situation (e.g., using circles instead of elaborate bracelets) because such drawings are easier to reflect on and save time for more mathematics learning.

Teacher Questions
- What information are we given in the problem? Explain what the 8 and 12 represent in the problem. Where in your drawing is each part of the information we are given?
- What equation could you write for this problem? Does your equation show the situation or your solution or both?

Student Assignment 2

Essential ideas: This problem also supports the grade 1 Focal Point of "Developing understandings of addition and subtraction and strategies for basic addition facts and related subtraction facts." In this problem, the number of bugs that Robin starts with is the unknown and the five bugs she gave to her brother are subtracted from the unknown to get the eight bugs that Robin kept for herself ($? - 5 = 8$). If a student just looks at the numbers and does not think about the situation, he or she may incorrectly subtract the 5 from the 8 and give an answer that Robin found three bugs ($8 - 5 = 3$). But if the student draws five circles for the bugs Robin gave to her brother and eight circles for bugs she kept to show at school, the student can see that he or she needs to put those bugs together (add them) to find out how many bugs Robin found in all. This approach also shows that some students may think of this problem as a separating rather than a change situation; Robin found some bugs and separated them into five bugs and eight bugs. Either way of thinking is fine, as long as a reasonable argument can be made to support it. So for this problem, a situation equation is $? - 5 = 8$ and a solution equation is $? = 5 + 8$ or $? = 8 + 5$. Many students think about the situation and write a situation equation and then solve it; they do not need to write a solution equation.

Teacher Questions
- What information are we given in the problem? Explain what the 8 and 12 represent in the problem. Where in your drawing is each part of the information we are given?
- What equation could you write for this problem? Does your equation show the situation or your solution or both?

Student Assignment 3

Essential ideas: This problem supports the Focal Points for prekindergarten–grade 2 related to geometry and identifying and describing two-dimensional shapes. The problem requires students to compare and contrast geometric figures to determine similarities and differences among them. Many examples of different triangles are shown as well as figures that are not triangles and ones that may share some but not all characteristics of triangles. A problem such as this can help distinguish students who have complete understanding of a triangle no matter its orientation, length of sides, size of angles, or closure of sides or angles from students who have incomplete understanding of triangles.

Teacher Questions
- How do you know the figure is (is not) a triangle?
- What do all the figures identified as triangles have in common?

Student Assignment 4

Essential ideas: This problem supports the grade 2 Focal Point of "Developing an understanding of linear measurement and facility in measuring lengths." Such a problem helps students develop understanding of linear measure as an iteration of units in which (a) the units must touch each other, (b) the units are of equal length, and (c) the length of the item being measured is inversely related to the number of units: the smaller the unit, the more iterations needed to cover a given length.

Teacher Questions

- How would you describe the length of one of Dad's footsteps? [3 units]

- How would you describe the length of one of Alisha's footsteps? [2 units]

- What is the total length of the rug when Dad measures it with his footsteps? [8 footsteps] What is the total length of the rug when Alisha measures it with her footsteps? [12 footsteps]

- Why is the number of footsteps fewer when Dad measures the rug with his footsteps? [8 big Dad footsteps versus 12 smaller Alisha footsteps]

- How would the total number of footsteps change if each of Alisha's footsteps was only 1 unit in length? [24 footsteps]

Correcting-Student-Error Task

Sample response: The standard algorithmic approach to subtracting multidigit numbers can make more sense to students if they relate the steps in the procedure to objects or drawings that show hundreds, tens, and ones (see the following figure). In part 1, the student circles the top number of 174 in the subtraction problem and draws a picture beside it to show the number 174 represented in hundreds, tens, and ones. Circling the top number helps students remember that they need to check each column to determine whether the top number is big enough to subtract the bottom number from it. Students enjoy calling the circle with a stick shown in the figure below a *magnifying glass* that helps them look at each place in the top number to determine whether they need to ungroup to get more in that place. Next, the student ungroups (or decomposes) as needed so that the bottom number can be subtracted from the top number in each column. Finally, in part 2, the student subtracts the bottom number from the top number in each place to solve the problem. The ungrouping in part 1 as well as the subtraction in each place in part 2 may be done from right to left as in the traditional manner or from left to right as in the example shown. Doing all needed ungrouping first helps avoid the typical error of subtracting the top number from the bottom number, which arises because students may ungroup in one place but because they are already in subtraction mode as they move to the next-left place, may just subtract and forget to check whether they need to ungroup. This ungroup-everywhere-first method also allows students to ungroup or subtract from the left, which many prefer. Some will instead ungroup or subtract from the right, which leads to interesting class discussions about why both methods work. A student's explanation to classmates for the example shown may be something like this: "I can subtract 1 hundred minus 0 hundreds in the hundreds column, so that's fine. Now I move to the tens column. I only have 7 tens, so I can't subtract 8 tens from that. So I have to ungroup 1 hundred into 10 tens, which gives me a total of 17 tens. I now can subtract 8 tens from 17 tens, so I'm fine in the tens column. Now I move to the ones column. I can't subtract 9 ones from 4 ones, so I need to ungroup again. I can ungroup 1 ten into 10 ones. Now I have 16 tens and 14 ones, and I am able to subtract the 9 ones from the 14 ones, so I'm good in the ones column. Now I can subtract the bottom number from the top number in each column." Eventually, students will not need to make mathematical drawings to solve a subtraction problem such as this and will be able to perform all the steps of ungrouping without a drawing. But initially a drawing will help students better understand the steps of the traditional algorithm and will prevent them from making the mistake of subtracting the top number from the bottom number.

Students should also be encouraged to use addition to check their answers to subtraction problems and can use mental mathematics strategies to determine whether their answer is reasonable. In the instance of the student who got an answer of 115 for the problem 174 – 89, the teacher might ask the student to use estimation or mental mathematics strategies to determine whether his or her answer seems reasonable. Mentally, a student might be able to reason that an answer of 115 to the subtraction problem is not reasonable, because 115 + 89 will result in a total more than 174 (e.g., I know that 100 plus 89 is 189, so 115 plus 89 is greater than 189).

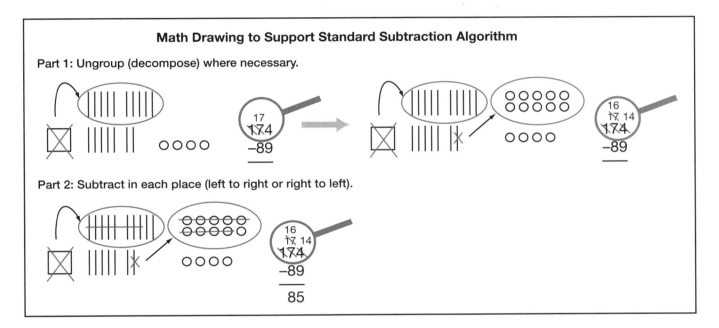

Developing-Depth-of-Understanding Task

Answers will vary. Appendix F identifies specific activities from the NCTM Navigations Series books that relate to the prekindergarten, kindergarten, grade 1, and grade 2 Focal Points.

Subtraction-with-Regrouping Task

See the answer to "How are basic facts and algorithms addressed in a focused curriculum?" beginning on page 11 and also the answer to the foregoing correcting-student-error task related to three-digit subtraction.

Professional-Development-Plan Task

Short-Term Goals

- Attend monthly meetings with my grade-level team to plan lessons and activities related to the identified Focal Point areas.

- Attend schoolwide and cross-grade-level meetings to discuss Focal Points and the growth of knowledge across the grades.
- Attend one or two professional development offerings or courses related to an identified Focal Point area for my grade level.

Long-Term Goals

- Continue to increase mathematics content knowledge by taking professional development offerings or courses related to the Focal Point areas for my grade level.
- Work with the principal and other school administrators to support new teachers in teaching a focused curriculum.
- Build a library of resources that support the teaching of a focused mathematics curriculum.

Sample-Student-Work Task

Bracelets Problem

Sample Work 1

The student understood the situation, was able to draw an accurate picture of the problem, and gave the correct answer of four more bracelets. The student, however, wrote an incorrect number sentence showing that 8 plus 12 is equal to 4. This situation is an unknown-addend problem in which the unknown, or the answer to the problem, is the number that the solver adds to 8 to get the total of 12 bracelets (8 + ? = 12). Students often think that the answer to a problem always has to appear after the equals sign, or underneath the horizontal line for problems written vertically. The teacher might cover up the 4 in the student's number sentence and have the student explain what the top half of the written notation means so that the student can see that the number sentence given does not make sense for the situation. The teacher might then point out the student's correctly drawn picture to represent the situation and ask, "How might we use numbers to show what you did in your picture." Many students spontaneously write correct a situation equation (8 + ? = 12) for this situation, but some may need to see equations of this type to understand that they can write such equations. Using a "mystery box" instead of a "?" is helpful to some students to show such situations: 8 + □ = 12.

Sample Work 2

The student seems to have understood of the situation. He or she gave the correct answer and wrote a correct number sentence. The student drew eight bracelets and on the basis of the sentence "4 to get to 12," counted on, "nine, ten, eleven, twelve," to determine that four more bracelets were needed. The student might be encouraged to label the equation to relate it to the situations (e.g., using such words as *made, need, in all*) and to make a mathematical drawing using circles instead of elaborate bracelets.

Sample Work 3
The student seems to have misunderstood the problem, thinking it says that Lisa needs to make twelve more bracelets in addition to the eight bracelets she already made. The student did accurately draw twenty bracelets to solve the problem 8 + 12 but may have miscounted when he or she added all the bracelets and so found 21 as the answer. Encouraging the student to make a simple mathematical drawing would decrease counting errors and save valuable time. The teacher might read through the problem sentence by sentence and help the student understand what the problem is asking. Other students might be asked to retell the story in their own words to help the student understand. For this student and others who may have difficulty representing the situation, the teacher might have students act out the problem. The most important step is to encourage students to understand the problem situation. This student may have heard the two numbers 8 and 12 and the words *all together* and assumed that those numbers needed to be added.

Packages-of-Gum Problem

Sample Work 1
The student was able to correctly draw a picture to represent the problem. The student knew that the total number of pieces of gum was fifteen but wrote an incorrect number sentence: 3 + 5 = 15. The teacher might cover up the 15 in the student's number sentence and ask the student to solve the problem 3 + 5. The teacher might have the student label each package of gum with the number of pieces in each (5) and then work with the student to come up with the appropriate number sentence to find the total (5 + 5 + 5 = 15). The teacher might first start with just two packages of gum and ask the student to write a number sentence to show the total number of pieces of gum in two packages (5 + 5 = 10).

Sample Work 2
The student correctly drew a picture to represent the problem but wrote an incorrect number sentence to represent the problem and came up with an incorrect answer of eight total pieces of gum. The teacher might have the student label the number of pieces of gum in each package that he or she drew and then work with the student to come up with the appropriate number sentence as described in the evaluation of sample work 1.

Sample Work 3
The student seems to have had a clear understanding of the problem; he or she was able to draw a picture to represent the situation and write a correct number sentence with the correct answer. The teacher might move on to helping this student write a multiplication equation: 3 × 5 = 15.

All-about-Triangles Problem

Sample Work 1
The student did identify all the figures that are triangles (figures 1, 5, and 10) and gave a correct definition but also included a few figures that are not triangles. Although the student stated that a triangle must be closed, he or she identified figure 7 as a triangle, possibly because the break in its side appears to be smaller than the break in the side of figure 4, which the student did not identify as a triangle. The teacher might ask the student to explain why

he or she identified figure 7 as a triangle but not figure 4. The student also noted that triangles must have three straight sides but identified figure 3, which has curved sides, as a triangle. The teacher might ask the student to explain why he or she identified figure 3 as a triangle but not figure 8.

Sample Work 2

The student evidenced strong understanding of triangles. He or she correctly identified only the three figures that are triangles and properly stated the characteristics of a triangle. To fully assess the student's knowledge, the teacher might ask the student to explain why each of the other figures is not a triangle.

Sample Work 3

The student showed an incomplete understanding of triangles. The student did identify the three figures that are triangles but also identified other figures that resemble triangles in some aspect. The student stated only one characteristic of triangles—that it has three "points" (or angles). The teacher might ask the student to tell how figures 3 and 8, which do not have straight sides, are different from, say, figures 1 and 5, which are triangles. To further develop the student's understanding of triangles, the teacher might cut out and paste each of the figures onto index cards and have the student sort the figures according to different attributes.

Footsteps Problem

Sample Work 1

The student gave the correct answers for the number of steps for Dad and Alisha, but the drawings of the footsteps were not exactly 3 units each for Dad's nor two units each for Alisha's. The teacher might ask the student the following questions to help develop the understanding of the need for equal-length units: How would you describe the length of one of Dad's footsteps? How would you describe the length of one of Alisha's footsteps? Does the length of each footstep change as Dad walks across the rug? Does the length of each footstep change as Alisha walks across the rug?

Sample Work 2

The student correctly drew three-unit footsteps for Dad and two-unit footsteps for Alisha and gave the correct answer for the total number of footsteps for each. To further assess the student's understanding related to linear measurement, the teacher might ask the following questions: Why is the number of footsteps needed to measure the length of the rug fewer when Dad measures it with his footsteps? How would the number of footsteps change if each of Alisha's footsteps was only 1 unit in length?

Sample Work 3

The student gave the correct answer for Alisha's total number of footsteps and drew an accurate picture, but incorrectly drew each of Dad's footsteps also as a two-unit step. Questions similar to those described in the evaluation of sample work 1 could be asked.

Measuring-Depth-of-Understanding Task

The following is a sample classroom scenario of assessing subtraction at the kindergarten level. Three students' solutions and explanations are given as well as an evaluation of the solutions, including ways that the teacher might extend students' understanding.

A teacher elicited addition and subtraction story problems from her class. Michael gave this problem: "My Dad got 6 oranges at the store. We ate 2 today. How many are left?" At this point in the year, the students were able to solve Michael's problem, and then three students explained their methods. The teacher wanted the class to see these three solutions because they show a range from less to more advanced.

Sample solution and explanation 1

Julia used counters for the oranges and did a take-away solution in three steps:

Step 1: *First I make 6 oranges*:   o o o o o o

Step 2: *Then I take away the 2 oranges they ate today*:   o o o o

[taken away and put somewhere else: o o]

Step 3: Now I count how many are left: o o o o

1 2 3 4   There are 4 left.

This student seems to have had a good understanding of the subtraction situation and was able to directly model it with objects to find the answer. She could be encouraged to write an expression to show the subtraction action: 6 – 2. Also, the first two steps of Julia's explanation connected her counters with the situation involving the oranges, but her last step did not. She might be asked, "Can you tell us what these four counters are in Michael's story?" [They are the four oranges his family still has.]

Sample solution and explanation 2

Sam used his fingers and also did a take-away solution in three steps:

Step 1: *I show 6 fingers for all of the oranges.*

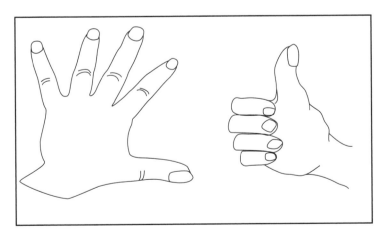

Step 2: *Now I put 2 fingers down.*

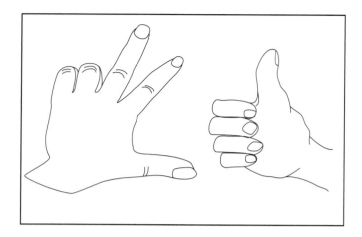

Step 3: *Now I see 4 fingers left. And I can write the subtraction* [writes 6 – 2].

The first step of Sam's explanation connected his fingers with the situation involving the oranges, but the last two steps did not. The class might be asked, "Can anyone ask Sam a question to help him explain more?" [What did putting down your two fingers mean in the story? What are your four fingers at the end in the story?] If Sam has just started writing expressions for subtraction, some positive comment is in order. If he has been doing so for a while, he might be encouraged to try to write the whole equation.

Sample solution and explanation 3
Asha made a mathematical drawing and wrote an equation. Having created the drawing, she needed to explain each step from the final drawing to allow everyone to see how the three parts of the subtraction situation related to one another.

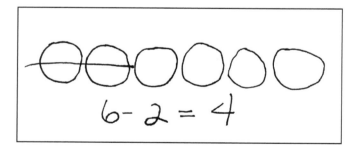

Asha explained her drawing as follows: "Here [pointing to all six of the circles] are the six oranges Michael's Dad bought at the store. Here [pointing to the two oranges crossed out] I crossed out the two they ate. And here [pointing to the four oranges not crossed out] are the four they have left to eat [pointing to her equation]. Six minus 2 equals 4. Does anyone have any questions?"

Students at this age typically model and solve a problem and then write the equation. In her approach to the oranges problem, Asha did just that—she made her drawing first and then wrote the equation. Her explanation fully related parts of her drawing to the situation with the oranges. Questions might be posed to Asha or to the class after her explanation to prompt students to find relationships across the solution methods, for example, "How are these solutions alike? How are they different?"

We can see here how the more advanced students in a class can model fuller solution methods and explanations for other students. Initially this modeling of more advanced approaches may have to come at least partially from the teacher, but the teacher should always begin by eliciting responses from students and then extending their work by questioning and then by example when needed.

References

Cavanagh, Mary, Linda Dacey, Carol R. Findell, Carole E. Greenes, Linda Jensen Sheffield, and Marian Small. *Navigating through Number and Operations in Prekindergarten–Grade 2.* Reston, Va.: National Council of Teachers of Mathematics, 2004.

Glanfield, Florence, William S. Bush, and Jean Kerr Stenmark, eds. *Mathematics Assessment: A Practical Handbook for Grades K–2.* Reston, Va.: National Council of Teachers of Mathematics, 2003.

Hiebert, James, Thomas P. Carpenter, Elizabeth Fennema, Karen C. Fuson, Diana Wearne, Hanlie Murray, Alwyn Olivier, and Piet Human. *Making Sense: Teaching and Learning Mathematics with Understanding.* Portsmouth, N.H.: Heinemann, 1997.

Huinker, DeAnn, ed. *Mathematics Assessment Sampler, Prekindergarten–Grade 2.* Reston, Va.: National Council of Teachers of Mathematics, 2006.

Ma, Liping. *Knowing and Teaching Elementary Mathematics: Teachers' Understanding of Fundamental Mathematics in China and the United States.* Mahwah, N.J.: Lawrence Erlbaum Associates, 1999.

Martin, Tami S., ed. *Mathematics Teaching Today: Improving Practice, Improving Student Learning,* 2nd ed. Reston, Va.: National Council of Teachers of Mathematics, 2007.

National Council of Teachers of Mathematics. *Curriculum and Evaluation Standards for School Mathematics.* Reston, Va.: NCTM, 1989.

———. *Principles and Standards for School Mathematics.* Reston, Va.: NCTM, 2000.

———. *Curriculum Focal Points for Prekindergarten through Grade 8 Mathematics: A Quest for Coherence.* Reston, Va.: NCTM, 2006.

National Mathematics Advisory Panel. "Learning Progresses Progress Report, September 2007." http://www.ed.gov/about/bdscomm/list/mathpanel/8th-meeting/presentations/progressreports.html.

Shulman, Lee S. "Those Who Understand: Knowledge Growth in Teaching." *Educational Researcher* 15 (February 1986): 4–14.